UNIVERSITY O

LIB/LEND/001

CARING AND EMPLOYME

by

Louise Corti, Heather Laurie and Shirley Dex

LONG
LOAN

The views expressed in the report are the authors' and do not
necessarily reflect those of the Department.

ED Research Series

The Employment Department is committed to promoting a competitive, efficient and flexible labour market so that Britain can compete effectively within the European Community and in wider world markets.

The Department has policies and programmes in place to help to achieve this goal. For example, to ensure that unemployed and other disadvantaged people have the skills and motivation they need to compete actively for jobs; to help improve the skills of the workforce and entrants to it; to maintain a framework which provides a fair balance between the interests of people at work and their employers; to protect people at work from industrial risks; to encourage employment patterns, practices and attitudes which promote individual choice and enterprise; and to promote the interests of women in the workplace and beyond.

To ensure that public money is well spent we must continue to monitor the extent to which the Department is achieving its aim and objectives. To do this we need systematic and impartial information on the operation of the labour market and the Department therefore funds a comprehensive range of research and evaluation work to complement regular labour market statistics.

The Department's Research Series makes the findings of these studies publicly available as a contribution to discussion and debate on improving the workings of the British labour market.

Richard Bartholomew
Chief Research Officer

CONTENTS

Summary

Introduction

The purpose of this report is to identify the demographic and socio-economic characteristics of individuals, and the households in which they live who look after a sick, handicapped or elderly person. The main aim is to examine the nature of the relationship between caring and employment. Prior to this report, the only large scale survey of carers to give estimates of caring and which describe characteristics of caring households was carried out by OPCS in 1985, as an addition to the GHS, sponsored by the Department of Health. A further national study was carried out by OPCS in 1986 on the prevalence of disability among adults in Britain. Data analysed in this report from the British Household Panel Study, provides an update on information about the situation of informal carers in Britain in 1991.

The analysis reported herein has been carried out by the ESRC Research Centre on Micro-Social Change based at the University of Essex on behalf of the Employment Department. The data are drawn from Wave 1 of the British Household Panel Study (BHPS), a national household panel survey of over 10,000 individuals in some 5,500 households in Britain. The sample was drawn from the small users file of the Postcode Address File and covers non-institutional residences in England, Wales and Scotland (north of the Caledonian Canal excluded). The BHPS is an annual survey which started in September 1991 and will return to re-interview panel members on an annual basis over the coming years.

At Wave 1 of the survey 13840 individuals were enumerated in 5511 households. Of these 9912 eligible adults were interviewed and 352 proxy interviews taken giving an upper response rate (full interviews with at least one member of the household) of 74%. For the purposes of the analysis reported here the sample consists of the 9912 respondents who answered a full individual questionnaire.[1]

Resident carers (Section A)

Carers were defined as individuals who were looking after or giving special help to anyone who was sick, handicapped or elderly either living in their own household, or outside the respondent's household.

The BHPS questionnaire contains a reasonably detailed set of questions about caring responsibilities or persons inside and outside the respondent's household, including how many persons they care for, the relationship to the care recipient, and how many hours were spent on caring duties, and whether the care recipient lived in an institution. The BHPS questionnaire also collects information about the whole household, and all adult household members, thereby allowing us to examine in detail the household characteristics of carers, the type of household they reside in, whether other household members are in employment and the financial situation of the carer's household.

In this report, the term 'co-resident' carer is used to denote caring for someone living with the respondent and 'extra-resident' carer is used to denote caring for someone not living with the respondent.

Our survey identified 1444 adults aged over 16, or 14.6% of the interviewed sample, who said they provided informal care for someone sick, disabled or elderly either inside or outside their own household. 1 in 5 households contained at least one carer.

Of the sample of all adults 4.4% cared for someone living with them, the majority of these caring for only one person inside their household. Of the 326 households identified containing a care recipient, one quarter contained two or more respondents caring for the dependent.

Of the sample of all adults 11% looked after someone not living with them, either in another private household or in an institution. One third of these respondents gave help to more than one person. Of the 885 households identified containing an extra-resident carer, a third contained two or more household members who said they provided extra-resident care.

Our estimates relating to co-resident carers differ very little from those reported in the 1985 GHS data, with the exception of our 1991 figures containing a greater proportion of carers aged over 65, and a greater number of men aged 75 or older who were co-resident carers.

Many carers were themselves elderly and caring for an elderly spouse, including a significant number of men, thus not conforming to the traditional stereotype of the female middle-age carer. According to demographic projections this situation is likely to become ever more predominant in the foreseeable future. We observed a greater proportion of individuals looking after parents than 1985 figures suggested. Of the carers identified, 18%

were caring for a parent and 13% caring for a sick or disabled child.

Of the co-resident carers a fifth lived in households containing a single couple and no children. Forty percent were in households containing 'a couple and other people' and a fifth in 'a couple and children only' households. Just under three quarters of carers were married, 12% were aged over 75 and 40% were aged 45-65.

Recent research tells us that women are more often than not the main carer of a dependent inside the household, and many of Britain's carers have to juggle the tasks of caring and paid employment. Our results suggested that caring was not an exclusively female task, but that there was an equal proportion of men and women caring for co-residents.

Care recipients identified in our sample were no more likely to be female than male and over half were 65 years of age or older, whilst one in ten was a child under the age of 16. One in six was married, and a quarter of the female recipients were widowed.

A third of the male co-resident carers identified in this report were retired, and a third were working full-time. Of non-married female carers, a third were in full-time employment, 7% in part-time employment, and over a third were looking after the home or family. Of the married women, 12% had a full-time job, 16% had a part-time job and 39% stayed at home.

Compared with all men of working age, 20% fewer male carers than other men worked in full-time jobs, but more were unemployed, looking after the home and family or the long term sick. Both married and non-married female carers were less likely to work full-time, and more likely to be looking after the home and family or the long term sick.

Many carers have to forego employment opportunities or change their working patterns to fit around their caring obligations. This in turn depends on the level of care required by the care recipient. For carers of working age, fewer male carers looking after their spouse had full-time jobs compared with all men of working age. Similarly, female carers looking after their spouse were far more likely to be looking after the home than all women. Of those caring for a parent or sick child, men were substantially more likely to be unemployed than all men, whilst a greater proportion of women stayed at home to look after the family.

BHPS data further reveals that carers had to forego employment opportunities or change their working patterns to fit around their caring obligations. A greater number of both male and female co-resident carers, than all adults of working age, reported having family responsibilities, including caring, which had prevented them from looking for a job, accepting a full-time job or having to leave paid employment.

Carers spending long hours caring for co-residents, were mostly identified as women looking after the home. Caring for a spouse entailed the most hours devoted to caring and caring for a parent the least.

The financial situation of caring households in the BHPS was generally found to be poorer than that of the general population, with household income clustering in the lower second quintile of the distribution, with some 40% having a gross income under £1075 a month. A similar picture of poorer well-being for carers and their households has been observed in other studies.

Of the carers 13% were receiving income support compared to 9% of all individuals, whilst over half of all households with someone caring for a sick or disabled child were receiving income support.

The distribution of occupations and social class of carers in employment further confirms other studies which have found a clear class gradient based on occupation, for the probability of being a carer. This is seen typically for both men and women, and particularly for those under the age of 44. BHPS data confirms that a disproportionate number of co-resident carers were in the manual occupations with twice as many in unskilled manual jobs.

Patterns of informal care in the community may be expected to undergo fairly radical changes in the forthcoming years. The timing of this report coincided with the first stages of the implementation of the 1990 NHS Care and Community Act (DH 1989, April 1993). Since the BHPS will be following the carers, care recipients and their households identified in this report over the next few years, the data will provide a very suitable vehicle for examining any consequences of this Act.

Child carers (Section B)

The main findings of the section of the caring report examining a) the characteristics and employment circumstances of respondents with dependent children (under 16 years of age) and b) the use and cost of childcare facilities where at least one child aged 12 or under was present in relation to both household and employment characteristics are summarised as follows:

Women's employment participation continues to be affected by childcare responsibilities. This is most marked when young children under the age of five are present but is also apparent in households where the youngest child is aged between 5 and 15 years.

Where children under five are present women tend to either withdraw completely from paid employment or to take on part-time rather than full-time employment.

Women's hours of work increase as children reach school age with 24% of women with children aged between 5 and 11 being in full-time employment compared to between 14% and 15% of those with pre-school age children. However, 46% of women with children of school age continue in part-time employment.

Some women with children under five are maintaining a presence in the labour market though mainly on a part-time basis. Of the 517 women with a youngest child aged two or under, 41% were in paid employment, 25% working fewer than 30 hours per week. Of the 200 women with a youngest child aged between three and four, 46% were in paid employment, 33% working fewer than 30 hours per week.

Women in current employment with dependent children have relatively low levels of monthly gross pay when compared with men which reflects both the occupations in which they are found and the hours they work. However, even when working full-time women with dependent children have monthly gross earnings significantly lower than those of men with dependent children who are working full-time.

Women with dependent children were less likely than men to be in professional occupations and were more likely than men to be in seasonal or temporary jobs.

Women were more likely than men to be working mornings or afternoons only or evenings or nights only. This provides some indication that couples with dependent children are arranging their working hours so that one partner is available to care for children when the other is at work. However, the data suggest that it is primarily women rather than men who are making these adjustments to the times of day they work.

Of all households with dependent children under 16 years, 45% were dual-earner households. Couple households with one parent earning comprised 28% of households, 16% were lone parent households and in 8% neither parent was in employment.

One of the most striking differences between household types was the mean level of monthly income, with dual-earner households being significantly better-off than other households. At the other end of the distribution lone parents who were not in employment and had children aged under five years had the lowest mean income of all households with dependent children. Home-based forms of childcare were most commonly used by respondents in current employment responsible for children aged 12 or under. On the first type of care mentioned 61% of respondents gave a home based type of care. The use of relatives or friends for childcare was also prevalent with 22% giving this as the type of care mentioned first. Only 13% of respondents gave an external/formal type of care as the type first mentioned.

The majority of respondents, 65%, reported using one type of care only although 35% did use two or three different types of care.

The age of the youngest child was significantly related to the type of childcare used. Where children under five were present an external/formal type of care such as a day nursery or a childminder was more likely to be used. Those using workplace nurseries comprised fewer than 1% of respondents using an external/formal type of care.

Those in professional occupations with higher earnings working full-time were most likely to use an external/formal type of childcare although home-based types of care were prevalent across all employment situations.

Respondents using external/formal types of care had the least traditional attitudes to women's role within the home and employment. Occupation and earnings were also related to the attitudes held with those in professional occupations with higher earnings being the least traditional in their attitudes to women's employment and family responsibilities.

Women were reported to be the main carer i.e. the person who cared for children when they were ill in 66% of households where the woman was in current employment. Those with more traditional attitudes were most likely to report the woman as the main carer but there was limited evidence of this responsibility shifting to the male partner where women held less traditional attitudes. In these cases there was a greater tendency for another carer such as a relative or childminder to be reported.

The majority of respondents, 83%, paid nothing for the type of childcare mentioned first either because it was home-based or provided free by a relative or friend. On the second type of childcare mentioned 75% did not pay for the care.

The use of a relative or friend to care for children was not always on an unpaid basis with 29% of those paying for their childcare using an external/informal type of care such as a relative or friend.

The amounts paid for external/informal types of care were significantly lower than for external/formal types of care.

Those with a youngest child under five and one child only were most likely to pay for their childcare.

Lone parents in employment with children under five were most likely to pay for childcare. 44% of lone parents with pre-school age children paid for some or all of their childcare compared to between 30% and 33% of couples with children in this age group.

Of those paying for their childcare the highest costs were being borne by those with children aged two years or under.

Whether or not childcare was paid or unpaid was related to occupation, level of earnings and hours worked with higher earners working full-time being most likely to pay for childcare.

The level of the individual earnings of the 'responsible adult' had a more significant effect than total household income on whether childcare was paid or unpaid.

In the majority of cases the 'responsible adult,' who in almost all cases was a woman, paid for childcare out of her own wages.

Footnote to Summary

1. Information collected by the proxy questionnaire did not cover caring for persons outside the household, and so proxies have been excluded from this analysis.

SECTION A - RESIDENT CARERS

1. Introduction

This section of the report provides information on the characteristics of individuals and households who provide informal care for an elderly, sick or disabled person in Britain in 1991. Two distinct caring situations are examined; where care is provided for a dependant inside the carer's own household and situations where informal care is provided to someone outside the household. The aims are twofold; first, to identify a range of characteristics of individuals who are carers and their households; and second, to look at how care providers combine their caring responsibilities with labour market participation.

Earlier studies

Up until now, the only readily accessible information on informal caring in Britain has been the 1985 General Household Survey (GHS) conducted by OPCS. Because so little was known about the numbers and characteristics of informal carers looking after a sick, disabled or elderly person, the Department of Health sponsored a series of questions in the 1985 GHS detailing aspects of caring. The resulting report *Informal Carers* (Green, 1988) provided valuable knowledge about the population of informal carers. A later study carried out by OPCS on the prevalence of disability among adults in Britain (Martin and White, 1988) added an important contribution to this knowledge. The analysis in this report provides up to date information from 1991 on the circumstances associated with individuals who provide care, and those in private households that receive care.

BHPS data

The design of the BHPS provides information not only about individual circumstances but also contextual information about the household in which individuals are living, and about other household members. In the study of informal caring, it is important to be able to identify dependants being cared for within a household, and to assess the domestic and household circumstances of carers.

For example, caring responsibilities may be important factors in determining an individual's decision to enter into paid employment outside the household.

The BHPS data allow these and other issues related to caring to be explored through an analysis of both household and individual level data. Although the panel will supply unique longitudinal information, the analysis reported here is based on the cross-sectional information collected at Wave 1 of the panel survey.

The analysis examines a broad range of characteristics of carers, and their household circumstances according to whether they care for those inside or outside the household. These include the distribution of carers according to age, gender, educational qualifications, marital status, employment status, income level and household composition. The carers identified in the BHPS sample are further classified by the relationship to their care recipient and by the amount of time they devote to caring.

Section 2 identifies households which contain carers and examines the prevalence of caring in Britain. Section 3 focuses on individuals caring for sick, disabled or elderly persons inside their own household and Section 4 on those who look after someone outside their own household. These sections examine the socio-demographic features of the carers and their households and identify the relationships of carers to care recipients. Section 5 reports on how much time carers devote to their caring activities in relation to whom they care for and whether other members of the household are also involved in giving help to the care recipient. Section 6 goes on to examine issues surrounding the employment of informal carers, particularly how they combine their caring activities with other roles, such as earning a living, participation in paid employment and taking responsibility for household tasks and so on. Section 6 also looks at constraints on carers' employment, and the employment situation of other household members, and carers' attitudes towards women's work and the family.

Defining carers and caring

There is no unified definition of informal caring, and there are very few surveys which have sought to unravel the complexities of a definition. 'Caring' in the informal sector is typically held to constitute care provided by family, friends, and neighbours, but not organised via a statutory or voluntary organisation, and which is not carried out for a financial reward.

Arber and Ginn (1992) suggest that the notion of a 'carer' has only been in widespread use since the 1980s.

OPCS carried out pilot work for the GHS to arrive at a suitable definition of caring, but their questions were limited by a space constraint in the questionnaire. The British Household Panel Study faced the same constraints. To enable a close comparison with the GHS, the caring questions designed for the BHPS are largely identical to those used by OPCS.

BHPS used two screening questions to identify those carers who are looking after someone living with them and those who provide care for persons not living in the household. The screening questions are asked only of respondents living in two or more person households. The questions are as follows:

Defining co-resident carers

Q Is there are anyone living with you who is sick, handicapped or elderly whom you look after or give special help to (for example, a sick or handicapped (or elderly) relative/husband/wife/ friend etc.)? If yes: Who is the person/people you look after? [ENTER PERSON NUMBER(S) FROM HOUSEHOLD GRID. (Up to 3 persons allowed)]

Defining extra-resident carers

Q Do you provide some regular service or help for any sick, handicapped or elderly person not living with you? [EXCLUDE HELP PROVIDED IN COURSE OF EMPLOYMENT] If yes: Is that one person or more than one? [IF MORE THAN ONE PROBE HOW MANY (7 OR MORE = 7) ENTER NUMBER CARED FOR]. Who is it that you look after or help? [CODE FIRST TWO MENTIONED. CODE RELATIONSHIP TO INFORMANT]

Codes: Parent/parent in law; Other relation (SPECIFY); Friend or neighbour; Client(s) of voluntary organisation; Other (Specify). Does (Dependant) usually live in any of the following:- hospital, an old people's or nursing home, or a home for the handicapped?

Another question was asked of all carers:

All carers

In total, how many hours do you spend each week looking after or helping (him/her/them)? [IF VARIES PROBE ' Is that usually under or over 20 hours per week'? INCLUDE CARE BOTH INSIDE AND OUTSIDE HOUSEHOLD]

The term 'dependant' in this report refers specifically to sick, disabled or elderly persons cared for by a respondent. It excludes children under 16 or in full-time education except in the case of a sick or disabled child.

Caring inside the household

Identifying 'caring' may be particularly problematic for intra-household caring situations, and ultimately depends on how the screening questions are interpreted by respondents. For example, elderly spouses may regard their usual daily living activities as caring for each other, but this may be in a symbiotic sense rather than in the sense of helping someone who cannot carry out normal daily activities by themselves. Furthermore, respondents who have been caring for a sick person for some length of time may not regard their caring duties to be over and above their usual family responsibilities. Hence the number of self-defined carers identified in this survey may vary from that obtained from a strictly objective definition.

In the following tables, those caring for someone inside the household, hereafter known as 'co-resident carers', are taken to be those who self-defined themselves as carers.

Care outside the household

Caring for persons outside the household will be referred to as 'extra-resident care'. Informal caring for individuals who are not residents of the carer's own household, covers a wide range of duties and services. 'Regular service or help' refers to practical tasks such as shopping errands for a neighbour. As other authors have pointed out for the GHS definition, this type of 'caring' activity has little to do with the dependency of the recipient and so the range of duties for this type of caring are more extensive than for co-resident care where 'normal' duties are excluded (Arber and Ginn 1992). As far as the possible the BHPS questions aim to elicit caring on a one-to-one basis rather than one-to-many (such as helping in a voluntary group). Piloting these questions did reveal that it was necessary to include a more rigorous definition of informal caring outside the household whereby interviewers were instructed to include only those caring duties which were primarily one-to-one relationships.

Type of care

The BHPS does not allow us to examine the kind of help that carers give to dependants. As noted above, looking after a dependant in one's household may embrace different caring tasks from those which would be given to someone in another private household or institution. The 1988 GHS report helped elucidate the range of duties and tasks undertaken by carers (Green, 1988). Help given to extra-resident dependants typically includes practical help with chores such as preparing meals or gardening, keeping company, taking out, helping with shopping and other errands and so on. Care to those outside the household will also involve travelling time to visit the dependant. Co-resident care, however, generally involves helping a dependant with personal care activities, such as washing and dressing, with nursing care, assisting with paperwork and financial matters and entertainment. It may also require continuous round the clock care, or being in attendance in case help is required. The latter type of care may place particularly heavy demands upon the care provider, particularly when they receive little if any support from other family members, little formal care support, or if they have to combine their caring roles with employment outside the household. Questions on the time spent caring in the BHPS provide a reasonably good proxy for the demands placed on carers.

Information about the care recipients

This report also examines some of the characteristics of individuals being cared for in the carer's household. The BHPS collected enumeration data about all members of the household, their ages, gender, relationship to other members, marital and employment statuses are available for each named dependent (identified by a personal identification number). Some named dependents, of course, were themselves interviewed, others had proxy data collected about them and some were not interviewed, either because they were under 16 years of age or unable to be interviewed for other reasons. For dependants outside the household the BHPS established only the relationship to the carer and whether they resided in a private household or an institution. Details of the time spent caring was collected as a total for all caring responsibilities.

Analysis of co-resident dependants' characteristics is carried out using information on them obtained from the household level enumeration data and is associated with the carer's individual interview data responses. Where carers were looking after more than one person in their household data are available for each named dependent. One caveat to bear in mind is that unlike the carers in the BHPS survey,

the dependants do not constitute a representative sample of 'dependents', simply because more than one carer may have reported the same member of the household as the dependent. For example, a husband and a wife may both report that they are looking after an elderly parent in their own home. When examining dependants' data, multiple mentions of the same dependant in the household by different household members who reported being carers, have been selected out to give a database of unique individuals who are care recipients.

2. The prevalence of informal caring and characteristics about carers' households

recipient. 16% of households contained at least one adult with caring responsibilities outside the household, and a fifth of these contained at least two such carers. 1% of all households contained someone who had dual caring roles of caring both inside and outside the household, the majority of which contained only a single carer.

Carers and numbers cared for

Altogether some 15% of adults reported looking after someone either inside or outside their own household (Table 2.1); 4.4% of adults reported looking after a dependant living in their own home, and 13% of these took on additional extra-resident caring tasks. The majority of carers looking after someone in their own home cared for one person, with just under 3% caring for two or more dependants. These figures are remarkably similar to those found by the 1985 GHS which revealed that 14% of adults had some caring responsibilities, and 4% were looking after a dependant in their own household (Green 1988). In 1985 this amounted to some 1.7 million adults caring for someone living with them and 6 million caring for a dependant(s) either inside or outside their own home. The sample size of the BHPS is relatively small compared to the 1985 GHS from which the caring data for the 1988 Informal Carers report was gathered. However the BHPS is a nationally representative sample of households in Britain which can provide an indication of trends in informal caring patterns in Britain from 1985 to 1991.

Just over one in ten adults reported giving help to someone sick, handicapped or elderly not living with them, either in another private household or in an institution. This figure is identical to the 1985 GHS estimate. Two thirds of these extra-resident carers looked after one person, and a fifth gave help to two recipients. 5% of the extra-resident carers also looked after dependants inside their own households.

Numbers of carers in household

Table 2.2 gives a breakdown of households containing carers. One in five households in Britain contained at least one person providing some form of informal care. 6% of all households contained at least one person who was looking after someone sick, handicapped or elderly in their own home, and a quarter of these households contained at least two 'inside' carers. The majority of households with at least two carers contained only a single care

Gender and age

Table 2.3 shows that 17% of women and 12% of men in the adult population said they looked after or gave special help to someone sick, elderly or disabled either inside or outside the household. Breakdown by age suggests that the 45-64 age group were most likely to be carers (19% and 27% respectively for men and women of this age group were carers). Moreover, the likelihood of being a co-resident carer increases with age for men (up to age 75) but peaks at 44-64 for women. Equal proportions of men and women aged over 16 define themselves as a co-resident carer (4%) but both gender and age differences are apparent. These figures are similar to 1985 GHS estimates suggesting that trends in the extent of caring has not changed dramatically, with the exception of a greater proportion of men over 65 caring for a co-resident (10% in 1991 compared to 6% in 1985). For the population aged over 75, 12% of men and 5% of women described themselves as co-resident carers, figures which are not revealed in the 1988 GHS report.

Women of all ages were more likely than men to be extra-resident carers. In the 45-65 age group, 14% of men and 22% of women were extra-resident carers. The 1985 GHS figures for this age group were 12% and 18% respectively pointing to a small increase.

Care recipients

Table 2.4 shows the percentage of all men and women caring for specific types of dependants. Of co-resident carers, the largest group was those caring for a spouse or someone aged 65 or over, and no gender difference are apparent. More adults in Britain look after a parent than any other type of dependant, the majority of parents living outside the carer's household. These figures are similar to the 1985 GHS figures, but as noted before, the BHPS probably under-estimates the percentage caring for an elderly co-resident parent, because the coding frame omitted parent-in-law.

Table 2.5 gives the proportion of households containing carers looking after particular types of

4

dependants inside and outside their own household. In 2% of all households someone was looking after their spouse, and of households containing someone caring for a parent or a child, just under two thirds contained two carers. 7% of all households contained at least one extra-resident carer looking after a parent, and in a quarter of these more than one person cared for a parent. 5% of households contained person(s) looking after friends or neighbours, the majority of which contained only one carer.

Table 2.6 shows that 18% of all co-resident carers lived in households in which at least one person had extra-resident caring responsibilities.

Characteristics of carers

Tables 2.7 and 2.8 show the demographic profile of carers. As we noted earlier, women are, in general, more likely to be carers than men. However, whilst the commonly held stereotype of a carer is one of a woman in her middle ages, the BHPS data suggests that co-resident carers are a heterogeneous group. Although almost twice as many of the extra-resident carers were women than men, co-resident carers were equally likely to be men or women. Of course, the balanced gender distribution of co-resident caring may not reflect the actual time spent caring for dependants. Time spent on caring activities is discussed later on in section 5. An age breakdown suggests that caring is undertaken by adults of all ages, with almost half of all extra-resident carers being aged 44-65, and co-resident carers being more evenly distributed across the age spectrum. One in seven male carers and one in ten female co-resident carers were aged over 75. Just under three quarters of all co-resident carers and 70% of extra-resident carers were married or cohabiting.

Household characteristics

In Tables 2.9 and 2.10 carers are classified according to household type. Just under one half of co-resident carers were resident in two person households, and a quarter in three person households. Lone carers predominantly resided in two person households, implying they were the sole carers of the only other household member (with the possible exception of external household members who may help). One in ten carers from two-carer households lived in two person households, these being households where respondents reported looking after each other (mainly elderly married couples). A quarter of lone extra-resident carers resided in single person

households, and 40% of two-carer households resided in two-person households.

Just under a fifth of co-resident carers lived in households containing a single couple with no children, a further fifth were from couple households with dependant children and 4% were from lone parent households[1]. 40% of co-resident carers were in households containing one couple plus other household members (e.g. other relatives or adult children). The distribution according to household type for extra-resident carers was very similar to the general population, but with fewer residing in households with dependant children. In multi-carer households, over half of both co-resident and extra-resident carers came from households containing at least one couple with no dependant children, and a third in both these groups from households with a couple plus children only.

Table 2.11 gives a breakdown of other household characteristics of carers. 13% of co-resident carers lived in households with two or more children, a quarter in households with two persons of working age and a third in households with two persons of pensionable age. Two thirds of co-resident carers owned or had a mortgage on their home, and a third rented their accommodation, the majority being local authority or housing association tenants. Very few co-resident carers lived in the private rented sector. Extra-resident carers had similar characteristics to the general population, but marginally more were outright home owners.

Financial characteristics

From Table 2.12 it can be seen that monthly household income[2] grouped into quintiles for the whole BHPS population, is not evenly distributed across co-resident carers. Co-resident carers tend to be poorer than the BHPS population; almost 30% of co-resident carers had a monthly household income between 572 and 1075 pounds, compared to only 16% of the population. The income distribution for extra-resident carers is not significantly different from that of the BHPS population. A quarter of co-resident carers lived in households where at least one person had claimed income support benefit in the last year, which is 10% higher than the figure for the general population.

We can examine the personal income of carers based on all sources of labour and non-labour income. A third of male and two thirds of female co-resident carers received less than 5000 pounds a year, which is substantially less than the population as a whole (21% of men and 49% of women respectively).

Moreover, the proportion of male carers in the top income quartile was half that of the whole population. It should, of course, be noted that the number of individuals with missing data for income are large enough to warrant caution when making these comparisons. However, although the financial well-being of these co-resident carers in part reflects the proportion being retired from paid work, 13% reported receiving income support benefit over the last 12 months. Section 6 looks in more depth at the employment situation of carers and their households.

Extra-resident carers were marginally, financially better off compared to all adults with almost 18% living in households having a gross monthly income of £2379 . Extra-resident carers were also much less likely to be receiving income support than co-resident carers.

Table 2.1   BHPS 1991: Percentage of adults who were carers and how many persons they cared for

	Adults aged 16 and over				
	Total care provision			Classified care provision	
	Freq	%		Freq	%
Provide care inside or outside household	1444	14.6			
Provide care inside own household	435	4.4			
			Cares for:		
			1 person	*423*	*97.2*
			2 people	*11*	*2.5*
			3 people	*1*	*0.3*
				435	*100.0*
Provide care outside the household	1066	10.8			
			Cares for:		
			1 person	*698*	*65.5*
			2 people	*208*	*19.5*
			3+ people	*120*	*11.3*
			missing	*40*	*3.7*
				1066	*100.0*
Provide care inside and outside household	57	0.6			
Provide care inside household only	378	3.8			
Provide care outside household only	1008	10.2			
			Cares for:		
			1 person	*656*	*65.1*
			2 people	*201*	*19.9*
			3+ people	*113*	*11.2*
			missing	*38*	*3.8*
				1008	*100.0*
Base = 100%[a]	9912				

[a] *Total excludes 352 cases who were interviewed by proxy.*

Table 2.2 BHPS 1991: Percentage of households with one or more carers

Households and adults aged 16 and over[a]

Carers in household	Total care provision				Classified care provision			
	Households		Individuals		Households		Individuals	
	Freq	%	Freq	%	Freq	Col %	Freq	Col %
At least one carer	1153	20.9	1444	14.6				
All co-resident carers								
At least 1 carer in household	326	5.9	435	4.4				
1 carer					239	73.3	243	55.7
2 carers					75	23.0	152	35.0
3 + carers					12	3.7	40	9.3
					326	100.0	435	100.0
Co-resident carers[b]								
At least 1 carer household	268	4.9	378	3.8				
1 carer					196	73.1	205	54.2
2 carers					65	24.3	140	37.1
3 + carers					7	2.6	33	8.7
					268	100.0	378	100.0
Carers providing both co- and extra-resident care								
At least 1 carer household	52	0.9	57	0.6				
1 carer					49	94.2	37	64.9
2+ carers					3	5.8	20	35.1
					52	100.0	57	100.0
Extra-resident carers only								
At least 1 carer household	885	16.1	1066	10.8				
1 person					701	79.2	686	64.4
2 people					177	20.0	356	33.4
3+ people					7	0.8	23	2.2
					885	100.0	1066	100.0
Base = 100%	5510		9912[a]					

[a] Total excludes 352 cases who were interviewed by proxy.

[b] Excludes those who also provide extra resident care.

7

Table 2.3   BHPS 1991: Percentage[a] of adults who were carers by age and gender

All adults aged 16 or over.

Ag1ring responsibilities	16-29		30-44		45-64		65-75		75+		All ages		All BHPS sample
	Men	*Women*	*Men*	*Women*	*Men*	*Women*	*Men*	*Women*	*Men*	*Women*	*Men*	*Women*	
Co-resident or extra-resident carers	6.1	7.4	9.1	16.3	18.8	27.1	16.8	17.5	17.6	12.1	12.2	16.8	14.6
Co-resident carers	1.7	1.7	3.2	4.1	5.7	6.6	7.4	5.6	11.7	5.2	4.4	4.4	4.4
Extra-resident carer	4.7	5.9	6.2	12.8	14.1	21.5	10.4	12.4	7.0	7.7	8.4	12.9	10.8
Base = 100%	1298	1277	1421	1435	1335	1386	458	587	265	44 5	4776	5730	9912

[a]   *Column percentage calculated on the base figures shown.*

8

Table 2.4   BHPS 1991: Percentage[a] of adults who were carers by gender.

All adults	Carers		
Care recipient	**Men**	**Women**	**All**
	%	%	%
Spouse inside household	2.1	2.1	2.1
Parent	4.9	6.7	5.8
Inside household[b]	0.8	0.9	0.9
Outside household	4.1	5.8	5.0
Child under 16 inside household	0.5	0.5	0.5
Person aged 65 or over inside household	2.5	2.2	2.4
Friend/neighbour outside household	2.2	3.5	2.9
Other relative outside household	1.8	2.7	2.2
Base = 100%	4777	5135	9912

[a]   Column percentages calculated on the base figures shown.

[b]   Excludes parents-in-law.

Table 2.5   BHPS 1991: Percentage[a] of households containing carers by type of dependant

Households containing co-resident carers

Number of co-resident carers	Care recipient							
	Parent		**Spouse**		**Child**		**Elderly**	
	Freq	**%**	**Freq**	**%**	**Freq**	**%**	**Freq**	**%**
All co-resident carers	21	0.4	105	1.9	28	0.5	107	1.9
1 carer		*38.1*		*81.9*		*39.3*		*71.0*
2+ carers		*61.9*		*18.1*		*60.7*		*29.0*
Base = 100%	5510		5510		5510		5510	

Households containing extra-resident carers

Number extra-resident carers	Care recipient									
	Parent		**Other relative**		**Friend/ neighbour**		**Voluntary client**		**Other**	
	Freq	**%**	**Freq**	**%**	**Freq**	**%**	**Freq**	**%**	**Freq**	**%**
All extra-resident carers	397	**7.2**	189	**3.4**	255	**4.6**	58	**1.1**	37	**0.7**
1 carer		74.3		83.1		89.4		89.7		100.0
2+ carers		25.7		16.9		10.6		10.3		-
Base = 100%	5510		5510		5510		5510		5510	

[a]   Column percentage calculated on the base figures shown.

Table 2.6   BHPS 1991: Co-resident carers and number of extra-resident carers in their households

Co-resident carers

Number of extra-resident carers in carer's household

	Freq	%
0	356	81.8
1	56	12.8
2+	23	5.4
Base = 100% Co-resident carer's	435	100.0

Table 2.7   BHPS 1991: Percentage[a] of all carers by gender, age, and marital status

All carers

	Co-resident carers %	Extra-resident carers %	All carers %	All adults %
Gender				
Men	47.8	37.7	40.4	48.2
Women	52.2	62.3	59.6	51.8
Age				
16-29	10.1	12.8	12.0	26.0
30-44	23.6	25.4	25.2	28.8
45-64	38.5	45.6	43.4	27.4
65-74	15.4	11.3	12.4	10.5
75+	12.4	4.9	7.0	7.3
Marital status				
Single	18.5	15.8	16.5	25.5
Married	71.5	67.9	68.6	58.7
Divorced/separated	5.9	7.4	7.1	7.6
Widowed	4.1	8.9	7.7	8.2
Base = 100%	435	1066	1444	9912

[a]   Column percentages; each variable of analysis calculated on the base figures shown.

Table 2.8   BHPS 1991: Percentage[a] of all carers by age and marital status by gender

All carers

	Co-resident carers %	Extra-resident carers %	All adults %
Men			
Age			
16-29	10.6	15.0	27.2
30-44	21.5	21.7	29.7
45-64	36.7	46.9	28.0
65-74	16.2	11.8	9.6
75+	15.0	4.6	5.5
Marital status			
Single	21.7	18.8	29.6
Married	70.5	72.3	60.7
Divorced/separated	5.5	6.3	6.3
Widowed	2.3	2.6	3.4
Base = 100%	208	402	4779
	%	%	%
Women			
Age			
16-29	9.7	11.4	24.9
30-44	25.5	27.7	28.0
45-64	40.5	44.8	27.0
65-74	14.4	11.0	11.4
75+	9.9	5.2	8.7
Marital status			
Single	15.5	13.7	21.6
Married	72.5	65.3	56.8
Divorced/separated	6.2	8.1	8.9
Widowed	5.8	12.9	12.7
Base = 100%	227	664	5132

[a]   *Column percentages; each variable of analysis calculated on the bases figure shown.*

11

Table 2.9   BHPS 1991: Household characteristics of co-resident carers[a]

Carers and adults aged over 16 in two or more person households

	Any carers		One carer	Two or more carers	All BHPSadults
			Number of co-resident carers in household		
	Freq	%	%	%	%
Household size					
2 people	194	44.5	73.1	10.8	38.4
3 people	110	25.2	12.6	52.0	23.5
4 people	66	15.2	8.1	24.5	24.2
5+ people	65	15.1	6.2	12.7	13.9
Type of household					
Couple no children	96	22.2	38.2	2.0	9.9
Couple with children <5	17	3.9	2.1	6.0	12.5
Couple with children 5-18	71	16.4	8.4	26.4	23.6
Lone parent + children	15	3.7	2.6	5.1	4.8
Other couple household	176	40.4	30.8	53.1	40.0
Other household[a]	58	13.5	17.9	7.5	9.2
Base = 100%	435		243	192	8580[b]

[a]   Column percentages; each variable of analysis calculated on the base figures shown.

[b]   Excludes adults in single person households.

[c]   The majority of these households contain either related or unrelated adults living together.

Table 2.10   BHPS 1991: Household characteristics of extra-resident carers[a]

Carers and adults aged over 16

	Any carers		One carer	Two or more carers	All adults
			Number of extra-resident carers in household		
	Freq	%	%	%	%
Household size					
1 person	174	16.3	25.4	-	13.4
2 people	375	35.2	32.3	40.6	33.2
3 people	222	20.8	18.6	24.8	20.3
4 people	199	18.6	16.9	21.6	21.0
5+ people	96	9.1	6.8	13.0	12.1
Type of household					
Single non-elderly household	77	7.3	11.3	-	5.9
Single elderly household	97	9.1	14.1	-	7.6
Couple no children	81	7.6	7.1	8.3	8.6
Couple with children <5	73	6.8	6.5	7.6	10.8
Couple with children 5-18	211	19.7	16.5	26.1	20.4
Lone parent + children	37	3.5	4.3	1.6	4.2
Other couple household	437	41.0	33.5	54.6	34.6
Other household[b]	53	5.0	6.7	1.8	7.9
Base = 100%	1066		686	379	9912

[a]   Column percentages; each variable of analysis calculated on the base figures shown.

[b]   The majority of these households contain either related or unrelated adults living together.

Table 2.11　BHPS 1991: Household characteristics of co-resident and extra-resident carers[a]

All carers

	Co-resident carers	Extra-resident carers	All adults
	%	%	%
Number of children in household <19			
0	77.6	71.7	66.5
1	9.1	13.3	15.0
2	7.1	10.8	12.9
3+	6.2	4.2	5.6
Number of working age in household			
0	23.8	16.7	16.3
1	19.8	15.3	14.3
2	30.8	41.1	42.5
3+	25.6	26.9	26.9
Number over pensionable age in household			
0	40.8	74.2	74.5
1	25.0	17.0	14.8
2+	34.2	8.8	10.7
Housing tenure			
Outright owners	33.9	27.2	22.5
Owned with mortgage	31.2	46.7	47.6
LA/HA tenants[b]	31.2	20.2	21.1
Other private renters	3.7	5.9	8.8
Base = 100%	435	1066	9912

[a]　*Column percentages; each variable analysis calculated on the base figures shown.*

[b]　*LA = Local Authority, HA = Housing Association.*

Table 2.12   BHPS 1991: Financial characteristics of co-resident and extra-resident carers[d]

All carers

	Co-resident carers	Extra-resident carers	All adults
	%	%	%
Gross monthly household income[a]			
(Quintile groups)			
£<572	10.7	13.2	14.1
£572-£1075	29.1	15.9	16.0
£1076-£1657	18.7	16.8	15.9
£1658-£2379	13.4	15.2	16.0
£>2379	12.4	18.4	16.7
Other (not specified)	15.7	20.5	21.3
Number of persons in household receiving income support[b]			
0	75.6	88.5	84.2
1	17.5	9.4	12.6
2+	6.9	2.1	3.2
Carer receiving income support			
On income support	13.3	6.8	9.9
Not on income support	86.7	93.2	90.1
Base = 100%	435	1066	9912

	Co-resident carers		Extra-resident carers		All adults	
	Men	Women	Men	Women	Men	Women
	%	%	%	%	%	%
Gross individual income (£ per year)[c]						
(Quartile groups)						
<5000	35.6	62.4	17.4	43.8	20.5	48.6
5000-<10000	25.8	14.0	18.6	22.0	18.0	19.6
10000-<15000	12.4	3.6	18.6	7.8	16.3	6.8
15000+	10.4	2.6	24.3	5.5	20.6	4.2
Other (not specified)	15.8	17.4	21.1	20.9	24.6	20.8
Base = 100%	207	227	402	664	4777	5135

[a]   Gross monthly household income refers to the total sum of all labour and non-labour income from all household members in the month prior to interview. Categorised into population based quintiles.

[b]   Receipt of income support refers to whether respondents received either income support benefit, combined unemployment benefit plus income support or family credit at any time during the last year.

[c]   Gross individual income refers to the total sum of labour and non-labour income for the last year, classified into quartiles for the whole adult sample.

[d]   Column percentages; each variable analysis calculated on the base figures shown.

14

Footnotes to Chapter 2

1. Dependant children are defined as under 16 or between the age of 16 and 19 in full-time education.

2. This variable refers to income derived from all sources of earned and unearned income from the month prior to interview gathered from all interviewed household members. The amount of missing data is relatively high for this variable; 16% of carers are not classified according to their household income. No assumptions can be made about this group, although whether or not they were themselves on income support benefit, and how many persons in their households received this benefit is a useful proxy for estimating how many carers fall short of the income support threshold.

3. Co-resident carers

The Tables in this section refer to those individuals who care for a sick, disabled or elderly person inside their own households.

Who are co-resident carers caring for?

As stated earlier, for the purposes of analysing the characteristics of dependents within households, multiple mentions of the same dependant have been selected out. 349 dependants were identified in the 5510 sampled households, however, as the sample of care recipients does not necessarily constitute a random sample, conclusions should not be drawn about the general population of care recipients.

Table 3.1 classifies dependants by gender, age and marital status. Approximately equal numbers of male and female care recipients were identified, but female recipients were generally older. Sixty percent of the women and under half of the men recipients were aged over 65, one in ten were children under the age of 16, and 30% were between the ages of 40 and 65. A greater proportion of male recipients were married or single than were their female counterparts, whereas almost a quarter of female recipients were widowed.

Some of the cell sizes in the following three tables are moderately small, so care should be used in drawing conclusions about carers in the general population.

Table 3.2 reveals that half of co-resident carers were looking after their spouse or a person aged 65 or over; 19% cared for a parent; and a further 12% for a sick or disabled dependant child. The distributions alter slightly when the number of other carers in the household is considered. In particular the proportion caring for a parent or spouse of those carers in two-carer households 24% cared for a parent and 22% cared for a sick child, whilst fewer (23%) cared for a spouse. Three times as many sole carers were looking after their spouses compared to those in multi-carer households and 15% more were caring for someone aged over 65 years old (mainly elderly spouses) compared to those in multi-carer households. The differences largely reflect the age of carers.

From Table 3.3 it can be seen that there are no significant gender differences in caring for specific types of dependants, although 8% more male than female carers looked after an elderly person in their own household. When we consider age of carers, Table 3.4 suggests that those under 30 were most likely to care for a parent or a sick dependant child, but very few of this age were caring for an elderly person. Of the 30-44 age group, a third looked after a person aged over 65, whilst a further fifth looked after their spouse. Of the 44-65 age range over two thirds cared for their spouse or someone over 65 (half of whom were a parent). Three quarters of those aged over 75 were caring for their elderly spouses.

Household characteristics and caring for specific types of dependants

Table 3.5 reflects variations in the household characteristics of carers and their dependants. Again the small cell sizes should be noted. Ten percent of those caring for a parent and two thirds of those caring for a child came from households with two or more children. Of those caring for a parent, a quarter lived in households with at least two persons aged over 65, and almost two thirds lived in households containing at least two people of working age. Those caring for children were twice as likely to be in households receiving income support than in other caring households.

Table 3.1   BHPS 1991: Percentage[a] of care recipients by gender, age and marital status

Care recipients inside the household

	All %	Men %	Women %
Age			
<16	9.7	9.5	10.0
16-39	8.6	10.6	6.7
40-64	29.2	34.2	24.4
65-74	23.8	22.4	24.4
75+	28.7	23.9	34.5
Marital status			
<16 years of age	9.7	9.5	10.0
Married/living together	60.2	63.4	56.7
Single	10.0	12.4	7.2
Divorced/separated	1.1	0.6	1.7
Widowed	19.0	14.1	24.4
Base = 100%[b]	349	170	179

[a] Column percentage; each variable of analysis to the base shown.

[b] Data base of all individual dependants, excludes 3 cases with missing data.

16

Table 3.2   BHPS 1991: Relationship of care recipient to co-resident carer in households

Co-resident carers

Relationship of recipient	Any carers		Number of co-resident carers in household		
			One carer	Two carers	Three or more carers
	Freq	%	%	%	%
Relationship					
Parent[a]	83	19.1	12.3	24.3	32.5
Father	31	7.2	32.9	9.9	17.5
Mother	55	12.7	9.5	15.8	15.0
Spouse	205	47.1	67.5	23.0	15.0
Own child	52	12.0	7.4	22.4	7.5
Any person aged over 65	235	54.0	58.8	41.4	50.0
Base = 100%[b]		435	243	152	40

[a]   Three of those caring for a parent, cared for both parents inside their household.

[b]   The column percentages to the base figures shown do not sum to 100% as some carers may care for more than one of the above types of care recipient in their household.

Table 3.3   BHPS 1991: Co-resident carers and who they care for by gender[a]

Co-resident carers

Relationship of recipient		Gender	
	All	Men	Women
	%	%	%
Parent	19.1	18.2	20.0
Father	7.2	6.8	7.6
Mother	12.7	12.7	12.7
Spouse	47.1	47.3	46.9
Own dependent child	12.0	11.7	12.4
Person aged over 65	54.0	57.7	50.7
Base = 100%	435	208	227

[a]   The column percentages to the base figures shown do not sum to 100% as some carers may care for more than one of the above types of care recipient in their household.

Table 3.4   BHPS 1991: Co-resident carers and who they care for by age[a]

Co-resident carers

Relationship of recipient	Age					
	16-29	30-44	45-64	65-74	75+	All
	%	%	%	%	%	%
Parent	45.4	27.2	28.1	0.9	-	19.1
Spouse	2.3	22.3	67.7	50.0	77.8	47.1
Dependent child	25.0	32.0	6.6	-	-	12.0
Person aged over 65	11.0	35.0	71.1	51.8	90.7	54.0
Base = 100%	44	103	121	114	54	435

[a]   The column percentages to the base figures shown do not sum to 100% as some carers may care for more than one of the above types of care recipient in their household.

Table 3.5   BHPS 1991: Household characteristics of co-resident carers by who they care for[a]

Co-resident carers

	Parent	Spouse	Retirement	Child <16[b]
	%	%	%	%
Number of children in household <19				
0	85.6	90.5	91.3	-
1	5.1	4.6	4.6	32.3
2 or more[c]	10.3	4.9	4.1	67.6
Number over pension age in household				
0	21.7	35.0	-	100.0
1	51.6	13.7	37.9	-
2 or more	26.7	51.3	62.1	-
Number of working age in household				
0	2.3	43.6	43.6	-
1	35.2	15.7	29.6	7.1
2	27.6	28.0	17.1	62.5
3 or more	34.9	12.6	9.7	30.4
Number on income support in household				
0	72.5	85.4	87.6	43.6
1	22.5	8.8	10.6	38.2
2 or more	5.0	5.9	1.8	18.2
Base = 100%	80	205	226	54

[a]   Column percentages; each variable of analysis to the base shown.

[b]   Refers only to a sick or disabled child.

[c]   Half of the carers in this group lived in households with three or more dependant children.

4. Extra-resident carers

The Tables in Section 4 refer to those who provide a regular service to or help someone not living in their own household, but living either in a private household or an institution.

Tables 4.1 shows that 83% extra-resident carers mentioned looking after or giving special help to someone living in a private household. Two thirds of carers were caring for one person only, and 7% reported caring for four people or more. (Table 4.2). Those caring for a recipient in an institution were more likely to care for two or more persons. The type of caring undertaken by these groups is most likely to involve visiting people in hospital, homes for the elderly or nursing homes etc.[1] Conversely, most of those helping a person in another private household did so for one person only. The gender differences observed are insignificant.

Who are extra-resident carers caring for?

Just under half of extra-resident carers cared for a parent and 27% of carers said they gave help to a friend or neighbour outside their own household[2] (Table 4.3). Marginally more men than women cared for a parent whilst other gender differences were not apparent. Married, separated and divorced carers were most likely to be caring for a parent, whilst more unmarried and widowed carers cared for friends and neighbours (Table 4.4). These patterns generally reflect the age of carers.

The majority of carers looked after a parent, relatives or friends and neighbours in private households, whereas half of those caring for a person in the voluntary sector or others did so for persons resident in institutions (Table 4.5).

Table 4.1 BHPS 1991: Extra-resident carers, and whether they care for someone in an institution or private household

Extra-resident carers

	Freq	%
Care for any person:		
In institution	150	14.1
In other private household	882	82.7
Not specified	34	3.2
	1066	100.0

Table 4.2 BHPS 1991: Percentage of extra-resident carers, number of persons they care for and whether they are in an institution or private households by gender[a]

Extra-resident carers

Number cared for	Any in institution[b]		All in private households		All
	Men	Women	Men	Women	
	%	%	%	%	%
1 person	48.8	53.0	70.6	71.0	68.0
2 people	12.3	17.2	20.8	21.5	20.4
3 people	8.3	6.8	4.3	4.0	4.7
4 or more people	30.6	23.0	4.3	3.5	6.9
Base = 100%[c]	54	93	337	542	1026

[a]   *Column percentage to the base shown.*

[b]   *Codes for place of residence were allowed for up to two dependents. This refers to either or both recipients mentioned being resident in an institution.*

[c]   *Forty cases missing are excluded.*

19

Table 4.3   BHPS 1991: Extra-resident carers and who they care for by gender

Extra-resident carers

Relationship of recipient	Men	Women	All	
	%	%	%	Freq
Parent	48.8	44.6	46.2	492
Friend/neighbour	26.4	26.8	26.6	284
Other Relative	19.9	21.2	20.8	221
Client of voluntary organisation	5.0	6.5	5.9	63
Other	4.4	2.9	3.4	36
Base = 100%[a]	402	664	1066	

[a]   *Column percentages do not sum to 100% since respondents may care for more than one of the above types of recipient.*

Table 4.4   BHPS 1991: Extra-resident carers and who they care for by marital status

Extra-resident carers

Relationship of recipient	Married	Single	Divorced/ separated	Widowed	All	
	%	%	%	%	%	Freq
Parent	57.8	16.5	34.2	19.9	46.2	492
Friend/neighbour	20.1	38.7	31.6	50.2	26.6	284
Other relative	18.3	31.1	25.3	17.4	20.8	221
Client of voluntary organisation	4.9	6.8	6.3	10.8	5.9	63
Other	2.0	8.9	6.1	4.2	3.4	36
Base = 100a	724	167	79	96	1066	

[a]   *Column percentages do not sum to 100% since respondents may care for more than one of the above types of recipient.*

Table 4.5   BHPS 1991: Who extra-resident carers looked after by whether they were in an institution or private household[a]

Extra-resident carers

Dependents Location	Parent	Relative	Relationship of recipient		Other	All
			Friend/ neighbour	Client of vol org.		
Dependents location	%	%	%	%	%	%
Any in institution[b]	9.8	17.3	10.8	49.8	56.6	14.3
In private household[c]	90.2	82.7	89.2	50.2	23.2	85.7
Base = 100%[d]	492	221	284	63	36	1026

[a]   *Column percentage to the base figures shown.*

[b]   *Codes for place of residence were allowed for up to two dependents. This refers to either or both recipients mentioned being resident in an institution.*

[c]   *Where there are two care recipients, this refers to both recorded recipients.*

[d]   *Forty cases missing are excluded*

Footnotes to Chapter 4

1. As noted earlier, for the purposes of this survey, extra-resident care was deemed to refer to caring on a one-to-one basis, rather than one-too-many as in group work. It is possible that a proportion of respondents may have included the one-to-many situation

2. 9% reported caring for two parents and 20% for two relatives.

5. Time spent caring for dependants

In this section we will examine the time carers actually devote to their caring activities. Other studies have found that it is women who generally carry the main responsibility of full-time informal care. In 1985 the GHS estimated that 10% of women compared to 6% of men were the 'main' carers of a dependant[1], but that the proportion spending over 20 hours a week caring was 3% for both men and women (Green, 1985)[2]. Women were more likely to help with personal care and nursing than men, whereas men were more likely to take the dependant out.

Table 5.1 shows the amount of time carers devoted to caring for dependants inside and outside their households. A third of all co-resident carers spent at least 50 hours per week caring for their dependant(s) whilst over half of extra-resident carers devoted less than 5 hours per week on caring activities. The 1985 GHS figures suggested a higher percentage of co-resident carers than BHPS who were devoting 50+ hours per week (45%), but very similar patterns for extra-resident carers. However, we should note the amount of missing BHPS data (15%) for the co-resident carers on time spent caring which may bias these figures.

Female carers spend more time than men caring for their dependants both inside and outside the household (Table 5.2). For those with live-in dependants, 41% of women devoted at least 50 hours per week to caring, compared to 28% of men, whilst almost two thirds of men who were extra-resident carers spent less than five hours caring compared to only half of women.

Table 5.3 shows the proportion of households containing 'full-time' (over 50 hours per week) co-resident carers. Of the 326 caring households, 31% of one carer households had the carer spending over 50 hours per week on caring, and 15% of two carer households contained both members saying they cared for over 50 hours per week.

As might be expected the extent of care varies according to the type of care recipient; those looking after a dependant spouse or sick or disabled child in their own home were most likely to be caring full-time (Table 5.4). For dependants outside the household, those caring for relatives, parents and

clients of voluntary organisations, spent longer hours caring, than those caring for friends or others not specified.

For the majority of care recipients inside the household it was not possible to ascertain information about the state of their health, because they were not interviewed. Their level of illness or disability would be expected to be strongly associated with the amount of care required. For example, the 1985 GHS data suggested that the proportion of time spent caring was greater for those caring for someone with a mental disability, particularly children.

Table 5.5 suggests that caring for a single person in a private household was more demanding on their time than caring for someone in an institution. However, the reverse was apparent when the carer looked after two or more people.

22

Table 5.1   BHPS 1991: Number of hours spent caring per week by whether dependent lived inside or outside the carer's household[a]

All carers

Hours spent caring per week	All carers	Co-resident carers	Extra-resident carers only	Both co- and extra-resident carers
	%	%	%	%
< 5 hours	44.4	17.1	56.0	35.6
5-9 hours	20.5	13.0	24.4	21.7
10-19 hours	15.6	16.3	14.3	20.0
20-49 hours	9.5	18.6	4.7	15.6
50+ hours	10.0	35.0	0.6	7.1
Base = 100%[b]	1360	372	816	56

[a]   Column percentages calculated on the base figures shown.

[b]   84 carers did not answer the question on hours spent caring, 63 of whom were co-residents. NOTE: Because of small numbers in some cells, the original BHPS question categories were recoded: 'varied less than 20 hours' as '10-19 hours'; 'varied more than 20 hours' as '20-49 hours'; and 'other times' as '5-9 hours'

Table 5.2   BHPS 1991: Number of hours spent caring per week for co-resident and extra-resident carers by gender[a]

All carers

Hours spent caring per week	All	Men	Women
	%	%	%
Co-resident[b]			
<5 hours	17.1	21.3	13.4
5-9 hours	13.0	12.6	13.3
10-19 hours	16.3	16.6	16.0
20-49 hours	18.6	21.4	16.3
50+ hours	35.0	28.2	41.1
Base = 100%	372	174	198
Extra-resident[c]			
<5 hours	54.7	62.7	49.9
5-9 hours	23.4	20.3	25.3
10-19 hours	15.4	12.0	17.4
20-49 hours	5.9	4.4	6.9
50+ hours	0.6	0.6	0.5
Base = 100%[d]	987	370	617

[a]   Column percentages; each variable of analysis calculated on the base figures shown.

[b]   includes those who are also extra-resident carers.

[c]   excludes those who are also co-resident carers.

[d]   84 carers did not answer the question on hours spent caring, 63 of whom were co-residents. NOTE: Because of small numbers in some cells, the original BHPS question categories were recoded: 'varied less than 20 hours' as '10-19 hours'; 'varied more than 20 hours' as '20-49 hours'; and 'other times' as '5-9 hours'.

23

Table 5.3   **BHPS 1991: Household containing those spending over 50 hours a week caring for dependants inside the household**[a]

Households containing co-resident carers

Number of carers in household spending 50+ hours per week caring	At least one carer	One carer	Two or more carers
	%	%	%
0	65.0	68.9	54.5
1	31.0	31.1	30.7
2	4.0	-	14.8
Base = 100%[b]	326	239	87

[a]   Column percentage calculated on the base figures shown.

[b]   Base figure refers to households rather than individuals

Table 5.4   **BHPS 1991: Number of hours per week spent caring for co-residents and extra-residents by relationship to dependant**[a]

Co-resident carers

Hours spent caring per week	Care recipient						
	Parent	Father	Mother	Spouse	Child	Retirement age	All
	%	%	%	%	%	%	%
<50 hours	75.0	66.7	80.6	58.5	64.9	59.9	65.0
50+ hours	25.0	33.3	19.4	41.7	35.1	40.1	35.0
Base = 100%b	70	25	46	177	42	210	372

Extra-resident carers

Hours spent caring per week	Care recipient				
	Parent	Relative	Friend/ neighbour	Client of vol. org[c]	Other	All
	%	%	%	%	%	%
<10 hours	71.1	76.9	88.0	80.6	94.4	75.5
10+ hours	18.9	23.1	12.0	19.4	5.6	24.6
Base = 100%b	490	221	283	62	36	1044

[a]   Column percentages calculated on the base figures shown.

[b]   84 carers did not answer the question on hours spent caring, 63 of whom were co-residents. NOTE: Because of small numbers in some cells, the categories 'varied less than 20 hours' were recoded as '10-19 hours'; 'varied more than 20 hours' as '20-49 hours'; and 'other times' as '5-9 hours'.

[c]   voluntary organisation

Table 5.5   BHPS 1991: Number of hours spent caring per week by extra-resident carers by whether dependant was in an institution[a]

Extra-resident carers   25

Hours spent caring per week	In institution		In private household only	
	Cares for 1 person	Cares for 2+ people	Cares for 1 person	Cares for 2+ people
	%	%	%	%
<10 hours	87.9	78.3	78.3	84.0
10+ hours	12.1	21.7	21.7	16.0
Base = 100%[b]	73	69	581	239

[a]   *Codes for place of residence were allowed for up to two dependents. This refers to either or both recipients mentioned being resident in an institution.*

[b]   *84 carers did not answer the question on hours spent caring, 63 of whom were co-residents. NOTE: Because of small numbers in some cells, the categories 'varied less than 20 hours' were recoded as '10-19 hours'; 'varied more than 20 hours' as '20-49 hours'; and 'other times' as '5-9 hours'.*

Footnotes to Chapter 5

1. The OPCS definition of 'main carer' refers to the sole carer or care provider spending the most time caring for the recipient in question.

2. These estimates refer to time spent caring for persons both inside and outside the household.

6. Employment and caring

This section examines a number of issues surrounding the employment situation of carers. First the employment position, including: hours of work, occupation, educational qualifications of carers, and the employment of other household members is examined; and for married carers, their spouse's employment status. Second, the analysis looks at the effects of caring responsibilities on the capacity to earn a living or desire to do certain types of jobs. Lastly, carers' attitudes towards work and women's roles and the allocation of household tasks in married or cohabiting households are examined.

Age and employment

Table 6.1 displays the employment status of co-resident and extra-resident carers of all ages by gender and, for women, marital status. The distributions differ markedly for co-resident and extra-resident carers, partly reflecting the age distribution of carers with co-resident carers being older than extra-resident carers. A third of all men and a quarter of married women who were co-resident carers were retired, whilst 38% of all women co-resident carers were looking after the home[1]. Married women co-resident carers were less likely to be in paid employment than their male and non-married counterparts, with over half being in part-time jobs.

For extra-resident carers the distribution of employment status for men and married women was almost identical to the adult population, but with a greater proportion men and non-married women being retired.

Working age groups' employment

Table 6.2 shows the distribution of employment status for carers of working age, thereby excluding 28% of co-resident carers and 16% of extra-resident carers above retirement age. Looking first at co-resident carers, only 62% of men were in paid employment compared to 77% of the BHPS male population aged 16-64, whilst twice as many male carers were working in part-time jobs than all men of working age. Furthermore, substantially more male carers were unemployed or long-term sick. Fewer female carers, whether married or non-married were in paid employment than all woman of working age

but female carers were more likely to be looking after the home or family. This finding suggests that caring responsibilities have a significant impact on the opportunity for women to participate in paid employment.

The employment patterns for extra-resident carers are more like those for the whole working population, with a few exceptions. Fewer non-married women held full-time jobs than non-married women in general, but they were more likely to hold part-time or self-employed jobs. Lastly, a greater proportion of men and non-married women who were extra-resident carers were retired compared to all adults of working age.

Working hours

Table 6.3 examines working hours for carers in paid employment. Women co-resident carers who were in employment tended to work similar hours, on average, to all women in the sample. A greater proportion of male co-resident carers worked under 30 hours per week in their main job compared to men in general. Similarly, a greater proportion of male and female extra resident carers in employment worked less than a 30 hour week than did all men and women in the BHPS.

Occupation and industry

Table 6.4 gives the distribution of the Registrar General's class schema based on occupation, the major occupational grouping and standard industrial classification of carers currently in employment.

Whilst recognising the relatively small sample sizes of co-resident carers in the BHPS in employment, we note a greater proportion of them being located in manual occupations compared to the population of all employees in the BHPS, with almost twice as many being in unskilled occupations. Employed extra-resident carers follow a similar occupational distribution to the employed population with slightly more being located in the managerial and technical occupations and fewer in the skilled manual occupations than the population.

Classifying carers in employment according to the 1991 Standard Occupational Classification (SOC)[2] (HMSO, 1991, Vol. 3) suggests that co-resident carers were more likely to be in the personal, sales and other grouping but were less likely to be in managerial or professional occupations compared to all employees (Table 6.4). The proportion of co-resident carers in clerical and other occupations was similar to all employees. The occupational distribution for extra-resident carers did not show much deviation from that of the general population in employment.

Classifying industry using 1980 Standard Industrial Classification (SIC)[3] (HMSO, 1980) places a greater proportion of co-resident carers in the manufacturing industries compared to all employees (Table 6.4). More extra-resident carers were located in service industries than were all employees but fewer were employed in the construction industries.

Educational qualifications

Table 6.5 shows the highest educational qualification obtained by carers by age. Of co-resident carers under the age of 45, significantly fewer held formal qualifications compared to the population as a whole. Of 16-29 age group, 35% of co-resident carers held no qualifications compared to only 20% for the whole population, whilst of the 30-44 age group, 67% of co-resident carers held no qualifications, compared with 42% of the whole population. Extra-resident carers under the age of 45 were similarly qualified to all adults under 45 whilst the proportion of carers having some qualifications was actually higher than all adults for those over the age of 65.

Care recipients

Table 6.6 looks further at the employment status of carers aged 16-64 according to whom they care for. Of those looking after a parent in the household, over twice as many men were unemployed compared to the male national average, whilst men caring for a sick or disabled child were three times more likely to be unemployed. Half as many men caring for a spouse had full-time jobs compared to all male employees, and a greater number were classified as long-term sick or early retired. Of women caring for a sick or disabled child only one in ten held full-time jobs, compared to 26% of all married women of working age, and over half of these women carers were looking after the home. Of women looking after a parent a similar proportion to all women aged 16-64 held full-time jobs.

Table 6.7 shows the employment status of care recipients in co-resident carer households. Not surprisingly, almost half of all persons being cared for were over retirement age; whilst 10% were children under the age of 16, 7% were in paid employment and 13% were looking after the home, the majority of whom were women over retirement age.

Employment of other household members

Table 6.8 examines the employment situation of other household members in carers' households according to the employment status of the carer. Household members over the age of 65 have been excluded from the table. Considering male and female carers together, half of co-resident carers and two-thirds of extra-resident carers were in paid employment. Just under half of employed co-residents lived in households where they were the sole earner, and a further 40% lived in two earner households. Of the 177 economically inactive co-resident carers, 60% lived in households with no wage earners and 30% lived in households with one wage earner. Three quarters of extra-residents in employment came from households containing at least one other working person, whilst of the 303 extra-resident carers not in employment, half lived in households with at least one wage earner.

Table 6.9 cross classifies the employment status of married or cohabiting co-resident carers' (aged 16 64) by the employment status of their spouse or partner. Those who were caring for their spouses have been excluded. The cell sizes in this table are very small and so should be interpreted with care. Of co-resident carers who were married, over half the men in employment had wives who were also working, whilst only one in six wives of non-working husbands were in paid employment. These patterns differ greatly from those observed for all men of working age, where a greater proportion of employed men had wives who did not hold jobs, and where inactive men were far more likely to have wives who worked. This suggests that male carers who are not able to work, rely on their wives' earning power. The majority of employed female carers had husbands who were economically active, and two thirds of female carers who were economically inactive had working husbands, these figures largely reflecting those of the whole sample of working age.

Employment status and time spent caring

Table 6.10 suggests that co-resident carers who were not in paid employment spent more time caring than those in employment, although attention should be drawn to the small cell sizes in this table. As discussed earlier, it is possible that carers who are retired or homemakers may regard a greater amount of their time as 'care', simply because they spent more time at home with their dependants.

A greater proportion of women than men spent twenty hours or more per week on their caring activities regardless of their employment status. However of the group of retired carers, men reported spending more time caring than women. The most striking finding is that women looking after the family or home were the group reporting the greatest amount of time spent on caring, with almost three quarters of these women spending twenty hours or more caring for their dependant(s).

Extra-resident carers showed a greater variation in the time they spent caring according to their employment status (Table 6.11). Of those working full-time or those who were retired, women spent more hours per week caring than did their male counterparts, whereas for those working part-time, more men than women spent at least ten hours or more per week caring. As with the co-resident carers, the group devoting most time to caring were women looking after the home.

Caring and perceived employment constraints

It is also important to examine carers' own perceptions of how their role as a carer effects their opportunities in the labour market. The BHPS includes measures of perceived constraints on employment, but not specifically in relation to caring for sick, elderly or disabled persons. Respondents of working age were asked whether household or family responsibilities had prevented them from looking for a job, accepting a full-time job, prevented them from or required them to change jobs, leave paid employment or work fewer hours, and if so to specify what responsibilities these were.[4]

Over a third of female co-resident carers said that family commitments had prevented them from looking for a job (Table 6.12). This proportion is twice that for the sample of all women of working age. Furthermore, compared to all working women, 4% more carers said they had not been able to accept a full-time job they had been offered, and twice as many said they had had to leave their jobs or cut down their working hours. The picture is similar for male carers. At least five times as many male carers said family responsibilities had prevented them from looking for a job, accepting a full-time job or working fewer hours compared to all working men. Twice as many male carers than all men of working age had been restricted in changing their jobs and three times as many had had to leave their jobs. Once again the small numbers in this table should be noted before definitive conclusions are drawn.

The proportions of extra-resident carers who reported that aspects of their employment situation were or had been effected by family responsibilities roughly matched those for the whole population, with a few minor exceptions. Three times more male carers than all men of working age said they had had to leave their jobs or they had been unable to change jobs because of family responsibilities.

Table 6.13 shows the proportion of carers mentioning 'caring for a sick, disabled or elderly person' as one of the reasons for restricting their employment position. For female co-resident carers, childcare was cited most often (48%), and this is likely to include 'caring for a sick or disabled child'. A further one in five mentioned 'caring for their spouse or partner' and one in four mentioned 'caring for a parent'. Male co-resident carers were most likely to give 'care of spouse or partner' as the main reason (37%,) whilst one in four mentioned 'caring for a parent'. On the whole, informal caring responsibilities were explicitly cited less frequently as employment constraints than other reasons (such as childcare). Extra-resident carers were still more likely to mention 'caring for parents or relatives' than all working adults.

Attitudes towards work and women's role and household allocation of tasks

Included in the BHPS Wave 1 self-completion questionnaire were a set of Likert scale items covering attitudes towards the family, work and women's employment. This analysis takes the percentage either agreeing or strongly agreeing with each of the following statements[5]:

a) A pre-school child is likely to suffer if his or her mother works

b) All in all, family life suffers when the woman has a full-time job

c) A woman and her family would all be happier if she goes out to work

d) Both the husband and the wife should contribute to the household

e) Having a full-time job is the best way for a woman to be an independent person

f) A husband's job is to earn money: a wife's is to look after the home and family

g) Children need a father to be as closely involved in their upbringing as the mother

h) Employers should make special arrangements to help mothers combine jobs and childcare

i) A single parent can bring up children as well as a couple.

Table 6.14 shows the attitudes of carers and of the whole BHPS sample. On the whole, male co-resident carers displayed more 'traditional', that is less egalitarian, attitudes towards many of the issues than did all men in the BHPS sample, although equal proportions agreed with statements (d) and (g). The most striking finding is that almost twice as many male carers than men overall felt that it was the husband's job to earn money and the wife's to stay at home. Female carers tended to be more liberal than all women in general on issues (c), (d) and (e) above relating to the benefits of working for a woman, but more traditional on issues concerning working mothers with young children. Like the male carers, a higher percentage of female carers than all men, agreed with the traditional view that it was the husband's job to earn the money and a wife's to stay at home.

It is more likely than not, some of these differences in carers' attitudes arise because of the skewed age distribution of the carers sample; that is, older people tend to have less egalitarian views.

Table 6.15 reports the proportion of male and female co-resident carers in married households who described themselves as being the person mainly responsible for various household tasks and responsibilities involving the organisation of household finances. Since the questions cannot be considered to be entirely objective, figures for both men and women have been reported.[6] The most noticeable difference between carers and the general population is that female co-resident carers reported tasks being shared to a lesser extent, than all women did. Male carers, however, were more likely to say they were mainly responsible for household tasks from all men; a finding which is perhaps not surprising given that many were caring for their spouses, and were based at home.

Table 6.1   BHPS 1991: Employment status of carers aged 16+ by employment status, gender and marital status (for women)[a]

All co-resident carers aged 16+

Employment status	Men %	Non-married women %	Married women %	All %
Full-time paid employment	30.5	32.0	11.8	23.7
Part-time paid employment[b]	6.8	6.8	16.9	10.7
Self-employed	6.7	-	3.5	4.5
Unemployed	10.4	5.2	1.7	6.4
Retired	33.1	8.7	25.5	26.7
Looking after the home	3.0	36.1	38.6	21.2
Other[c]	9.5	11.1	2.0	6.8
Base = 100%	208	62	165	435

All extra-resident carers aged 16+

Employment status	Men %	Non-married women %	Married women %	All %
Full-time paid employment	49.2	25.8	23.8	24.4
Part-time paid employment[b]	4.5	11.9	31.7	24.9
Self-employed	12.8	4.9	7.4	6.5
Unemployed	7.8	6.0	.9	2.7
Retired	18.5	30.5	12.2	18.6
Looking after the home	1.1	14.0	21.5	18.9
Other[c]	6.1	6.9	2.5	4.0
Base = 100%	402	230	433	1066

All adults aged 16+

Employment status	Men %	Non-married women %	Married women %	All %
Full-time paid employment	50.9	32.9	24.4	39.0
Part-time paid employment[b]	3.4	9.1	27.1	11.8
Self-employed	12.3	2.3	5.0	7.9
Unemployed	8.2	5.0	1.6	5.5
Retired	15.7	24.6	14.1	17.3
Looking after the home	0.3	15.3	25.5	11.0
Other[c]	9.2	10.8	1.6	7.5
Base = 100%	4777	2216	2911	9904

[a] Column percentage calculated on the base figures shown.

[b] Part-time employment is defined as working 30 hours or less per week.

[c] Other category includes those in full-time education and long-term sick

Table 6.2   BHPS 1991: Employment status of carers aged 16-64 by employment status, gender and marital status (for women)[a]

All co-resident carers aged 16-64

Employment status	Men %	Non-married women %	Married women %	All %
Full-time paid employment	43.8	36.9	16.5	32.2
Part-time paid employment[b]	8.7	7.8	23.7	14.1
Self-employed	9.8	-	4.9	6.2
Unemployed	15.2	6.0	2.4	8.8
Retired	5.8	1.6	9.7	6.5
Looking after the home	3.6	34.8	40.1	22.6
Long-term sick	11.1	7.0	1.9	7.0
Other[c]	2.0	5.8	.8	2.6
Base = 100%	142	54	118	314

All extra-resident carers aged 16-64

Employment status	Men %	Non-married women %	Married women %	All %
Full-time paid employment	58.9	36.0	26.0	40.3
Part-time paid employment[b]	4.5	16.6	34.2	19.7
Self-employed	13.1	6.9	7.7	9.5
Unemployed	8.9	8.4	1.0	5.4
Retired	6.5	12.3	6.4	7.5
Looking after the home	0.9	10.2	22.0	11.9
Long-term sick	3.3	4.7	2.3	3.2
Other[c]	3.9	4.8	.4	2.5
Base = 100%	336	165	392	893

All adults aged 16-64

Employment status	Men %	Non-married women %	Married women %	All %
Full-time paid employment	59.8	45.9	28.3	47.4
Part-time paid employmentb	3.4	12.1	31.0	13.6
Self-employed	13.9	3.1	5.6	9.2
Unemployed	9.5	7.0	1.9	6.6
Retired	2.7	4.6	5.4	4.0
Looking after the home	0.3	13.2	25.3	10.5
Long term sick	3.6	3.0	1.7	2.9
Otherc	6.8	11.1	0.8	5.8
Base = 100%	4046	1583	2509	8138

[a]   *Column percentage calculated on the base figures shown.*

[b]   *Part-time employment is defined as working 30 hours or less per week.*

[c]   *Other category includes those in full-time education and long-term sick*

Table 6.3   BHPS 1991: Working hours per week for carers in paid employment by gender[a]

Co-resident carers

Hours per week	Men %	Women %	All %
< 30 hours	14.4	43.5	28.3
30-40 hours	53.4	43.5	49.4
41+ hours	31.2	13.0	22.9
Base = 100%	77	90	197

Extra-resident carers

Hours per week	Men %	Women %	All %
< 30 hours	8.9	48.7	32.2
30-40 hours	58.4	37.1	45.9
41+ hours	32.7	14.2	21.9
Base = 100%	380	269	649

All employed adults

Hours per week	Men %	Women %	All %
< 30 hours	7.0	42.2	22.9
30-40 hours	60.6	46.4	54.2
41+ hours	32.4	11.4	22.9
Base = 100%	3242	2675	5917

[a]   Column percentage calculated on the base figures shown.

Table 6.4   BHPS 1991: Distribution of social class[a], standard occupational classification (SOC)[b] and standard industrial classification (SIC)[c] for carers[d]

All carers in paid employment

Social class (Registrar General's)	Co-resident carers %	Extra-resident carers %	All employees %
I	5.2	4.1	5.4
II	20.5	31.9	27.4
III	17.8	24.8	25.1
IV	29.2	18.8	23.0
V	17.0	14.6	14.3
VI	10.3	5.8	4.8
Base = 100%[e]	165	630	5763

Occupation SOC major group	Co-resident carers %	Extra-resident carers %	All employees %
Managerial & professional	24.4	35.0	32.7
Clerical & craft	33.5	28.5	32.4
Personal, sales and other	42.1	36.5	34.9
Base = 100%[e]	165	630	5780

Industry aggregated SIC group	Co-resident carers %	Extra-resident carers %	All employees %
Energy	2.4	3.5	4.1
Manufacturing	28.0	20.9	22.8
Construction	6.4	2.9	5.8
Services	63.2	72.7	67.3
Base = 100%e	165	630	5759

[a]   Registrar General's classification.

　　　　Social class I   - professional occupations,

　　　　　　　　II   - managerial and technical occupations,

　　　　　　　　III   - skilled non-manual occupations,

　　　　　　　　IV   - skilled manual occupations,

　　　　　　　　V   - partly skilled occupations,

　　　　　　　　VI   - unskilled occupations.

[b]   Recoded SOC Major Groups. See Appendix A.

[c]   Recoded major SIC Groups. See Appendix B.

[d]   Column percentages calculated on the base figures shown.

[e]   Totals exclude missing information for social class, SOC and SIC.

Table 6.5   BHPS 1991: Highest educational qualification of carers by age[a]

Co-resident carers

Highest education qualifications	Age					Total	All BHPS adults
	16-29	30-44	44-59	60-74	75+		
	%	%	%	%	%	%	%
A-level or higher	19.4	10.8	23.5	13.6	13.4	16.2	22.3
O-level or CSEs	46.0	22.1	13.9	7.4	11.5	17.1	27.3
No qualifications	34.6	67.1	62.6	79.0	75.1	66.7	50.4
Base = 100%	44	103	121	114	54	435	9906

Extra-resident carers

Highest education qualifications	Age					Total	All BHPS adults
	16-29	30-44	44-59	60-74	75+		
	%	%	%	%	%	%	%
A-level or higher	26.3	27.2	19.6	17.3	8.4	21.3	22.3
O-level or CSEs	52.9	34.7	17.1	13.4	14.9	25.3	27.3
No qualifications	20.8	38.1	63.3	69.3	76.7	53.4	50.4
Base = 100%	136	271	391	216	53	1066	9906

All adults

Highest education qualifications	Age					All BHPS adults
	16-29	30-44	44-59	60-74	75+	
	%	%	%	%	%	%
A-level or higher	30.2	28.6	17.1	10.2	7.0	22.4
O-level or CSEs	49.8	29.5	15.4	10.4	6.5	27.2
No qualifications	20.0	41.9	67.5	79.4	86.5	50.4
Base = 100%	2574	2856	2720	1045	709	9906

[a]   *Column percentages calculated on the base figures shown.*

34

Table 6.6   BHPS 1991: Employment status of co-resident carers by relationship to care recipient by gender[a]

Co-resident carers aged 16-64

Employment status	Relationship of care recipient to carer					
	Parent	Child	Spouse	Retirement age	All	All BHPS adults
	%	%	%	%	%	%
Men						
Full-time emp.	49.0	49.5	27.0	36.2	43.7	59.8
Part-time/self emp.	12.6	15.8	22.7	24.2	18.3	17.2
Unemployed	19.7	26.1	7.0	13.6	15.1	9.5
Other[b]	18.7	8.6	43.3	26.0	23.2	13.5
Base = 100%	38	24	43	60	143	4046
	%	%	%	%	%	%
Women						
Full-time emp.	38.1	10.7	18.2	25.9	22.9	35.0
Part-time/self emp.	16.5	29.4	26.8	17.9	22.0	28.4
Looking after family/home	29.5	56.6	33.2	38.4	38.4	20.6
Other[c]	15.9	3.3	21.8	17.8	16.7	16.0
Base = 100%	45	28	63	67	172	4098

[a]   Column percentages calculated on the base figures shown.

[b]   Other category includes those who are retired, long term sick or disabled, and a small number of men looking after the home.

[c]   Other category includes those who are retired, long term sick or disabled and a small number of unemployed women.

Table 6.7   BHPS 1991: Employment status of care recipients[a]

Care recipients inside co-resident carers' households

Employment status	All
<16 years of age	10.0
Working (paid employment)	6.6
Unemployed	4.9
Retired	46.5
Looking after family/home	13.1
In full-time education	0.9
Other[b]	18.0
Base = 100%[c]	349

[a]   Column percentage calculated on the base shown.

[b]   Other category includes those who are long term sick or disabled.

[c]   Base of all individual dependants, excludes three cases with missing data.

35

Table 6.8   BHPS 1991: Employment status of household members in carers' households[a]

Carers aged 16-64

Number in household in employment[b]	Co-residents carers			Extra-resident carers			All BHPS adults
	In paid emp.	Not in emp.	All emp.	In paid emp.	Not in emp.	All	
	%	%	%	%	%	%	%
None	1.8	59.4	31.3	1.0	43.6	14.8	14.6
One	45.1	29.9	37.3	26.5	39.7	30.8	29.8
Two	39.9	8.9	24.0	51.5	14.7	39.6	40.2
Three	11.6	1.8	6.6	15.4	1.0	10.7	11.1
Four	1.7	-	0.8	5.6	1.0	4.1	4.3
Base = 100%	168	177	345	628	303	931	8509

[a]   Column percentage calculated on the base figures shown.

[b]   Includes only persons of working age, 16-64.

Table 6.9   BHPS 1991: Spouse/partners employment status by carer's employment status by gender[a]

Married or cohabitating co-resident carers aged 16-64 (excluding those who care for their spouse)

Spouse's employment status	Male carers		Female carers	
	Employed	Not employed	Employed	Not employed
Employed	54.9	17.5	92.8	68.5
Not employed	45.1	82.5	7.2	31.5
Base = 100%	36	11	27	31

All adults aged 16-64

Spouse's employment status	Male carers		Female carers	
	Employed	Not employed	Employed	Not employed
Employed	73.6	38.0	90.0	65.6
Not employed	26.4	62.0	10.0	34.4
Base = 100%	2223	440	1841	944

[a]   Column percentages calculated on the base figure shown

Table 6.10   BHPS 1991: Time spent caring per week by employment status of co-resident carers by gender

Co-resident carers

Hours spent caring	Employment status of co-resident carers											
	Full-time[a]		Part-time		Retired		Homemaker		Other[b]		All
Cares for:	M	W	M	W	M	W	M	W	M	W	
<20 hours	61.2	59.6	72.0	68.8	36.8	41.9	40.0	25.7	38.2	35.7	46.4
20+ hours	38.8	40.4	28.0	31.2	63.2	58.1	60.0	74.3	61.8	64.3	53.6
Base = 100%[c]	53	34	25	32	57	43	5	74	34	14	372

[a]   Part-time includes self-employed

[b]   Other category includes unemployed, long term sick, and other

[c]   Excludes 63 cases who did not report time spent caring.

M   Men

W   Women

Table 6.11   BHPS 1991: Time spent caring per week by employment status of extra-resident carers by gender

Extra-resident carers, excluding all co-resident carers

Hours spent caring	Employment status of co-resident carers											
	Full-time[a]		Part-time		Retired		Homemaker		Other[b]		All
Cares for:	M	W	M	W	M	W	M	W	M	W	
<10 hours	86.4	81.0	83.3	79.6	79.1	71.9	100.0	67.8	76.5	78.0	78.1
10+ hours	13.6	19.0	16.7	20.4	20.9	28.1	-	32.2	23.5	22.0	21.9
Base = 100%c	187	154	66	186	65	117	1	109	51	41	987

[a]   Part-time includes self-employed

[b]   Other category includes unemployed, long term sick, and other

[c]   Excludes 22 cases who did not report time spent caring.

M   Men

W   Women

Table 6.12   BHPS 1991: Percentage of carers agreeing that family responsibilities had an effect on employment situation in the past year by gender[a]

All carers; women aged 16-60 and men aged 16-64

Constraints on employment	Co-resident carers		Extra-resident carers		All adults	
	Men	Women	Men	Women	Men	Women
Family responsibilities	%	%	%	%	%	%
Prevented from looking for a job	15.4	36.7	3.8	16.1	2.4	17.2
Prevented from accepting a full-time job offer	6.9	12.0	1.5	8.7	1.0	7.9
Prevented from changing jobs	4.2	6.0	3.0	8.0	2.4	6.2
Required to change job	1.4	1.3	2.4	2.8	.9	2.0
Required to leave paid employment	1.4	8.7	1.2	2.8	.4	4.2
Required to work fewer hours	6.3	8.0	2.1	5.6	1.3	4.6
Base = 100%	143	150	338	502	3955	3762

[a]   Column percentages calculated on the base figures shown

Table 6.13   BHPS 1991: Percentage of carers mentioning caring responsibilities affecting employment situation in the past year by gender

Carers (women aged 16-60 and men aged 16-64) who reported household or family responsibilities effecting their employment

Caring responsibility	Co-resident carers		Extra-resident carers		All adults	
	Men	Women	Men	Women	Men	Women
Responsibility	%	%	%	%	%	%
Children/ childcare	33.3	47.6	16.7	58.0	21.8	70.8
Care of spouse/partner	36.7	19.0	-	-	11.7	2.3
Care of parents	23.3	23.8	12.5	15.2	8.7	4.6
Care of other relatives	-	3.2	4.2	4.5	1.1	1.5
General family care	3.3	3.2	8.3	5.4	6.8	3.5
Other[a]	-	-	58.3	16.9	49.9	17.3
Base = 100%[b]	30	63	24	112	206	884

[a]   Other category includes; divorce/ separation, personal ill health/ sickness/ disability; financial constraints or responsibilities; working in family business/helping spouse in job etc.

[b]   The totals refer to the number answering yes to any of the questions listed in Table 6.12.

Table 6.14   BHPS 1991: Co-resident carers' attitudes towards work and women's role by gender

Co-resident carers

Agree or strongly agree	Carers		All BHPS sample	
	Men	Women	Men	Women
	%	%	%	%
Pre-school child suffers if mother works	67.5	52.3	56.2	43.3
Family suffers if woman works full-time	54.5	40.2	43.1	38.8
Woman and family are happier if she works	14.5	26.2	19.4	20.3
Husband and wife should both contribute	55.0	64.0	52.3	58.0
Fulltime job makes woman independent	89.0	53.7	47.3	45.8
Husbands should earn, wife stay at home	50.5	33.6	29.0	24.3
Children need father as much as mother	94.5	92.1	90.7	87.6
Employers should help with child care	68.0	77.1	74.3	78.9
Single parents are as good as couples	28.0	43.9	30.1	46.5
Base = 100%[a]	198	214	4669	4982

[a]   *Total answering the self-completion questionnaire.*

Table 6.15 BHPS 1991: Allocation of household tasks and organisation of household finances for co-resident carer couples by gender

Co-resident carers in couple households only

	Co-resident carers		All BHPS sample	
	Men	Women	Men	Women
	%	%	%	%
Who is mainly responsible for:				
the grocery shopping				
Mostly self	37.5	60.5	10.9	53.1
Shared	32.9	29.3	40.7	37.0
the cooking				
Mostly self	23.7	86.8	9.7	74.2
Shared	27.1	10.8	21.4	18.9
the cleaning				
Mostly self	31.6	67.7	7.2	68.0
Shared	23.0	18.6	27.4	22.2
the washing/ironing				
Mostly self	19.1	87.4	4.9	84.4
Shared	19.1	7.8	13.3	10.9
the household bills				
Mostly self	52.0	52.1	39.7	47.2
Shared	13.1	14.9	16.9	16.5
the housekeeping				
Mostly self	28.9	85.6	8.9	79.0
Shared	13.8	9.0	16.4	13.7
Base = 100%[a]	152	167	3181	3185

[a] *Total refers to couple households only.*

Footnotes to Chapter 6

1. Since employment status in this case is self-defined, a number of women over the statutory retirement age defined themselves as 'looking after the home' instead of 'retired'.

2. Respondents occupations in the BHPS were coded to the 1991 Standard Occupational Classification (SOC) (HMSO, 1991, Vol.3). Carers were classified according to the nine major SOC occupational groups listed in Appendix A

3. The BHPS data were coded to the 1980 Standard Industrial Classification (SIC) (CSO, HMSO, 1980 (revised)). For carers, the ten major SIC divisions were aggregated as in Appendix B.

4. Interviewers recorded an open-ended verbatim reply from respondents which was office coded to a detailed frame. The codes included 'family responsibilities' (such as those pertaining to childcare, personal health, and financial circumstances), informal care, care of spouse or partner; care of parents, elderly/ sick; care of other relatives; care of non-relatives. The six questions on constraints on employment can therefore be said to cover informal care.

5. The response set was a five point scale ranging from strongly agree to strongly disagree.

6. A picture of the 'true' situation would reveal distributions for men and women that are identical for the 'sharing' response, and that roughly sum to 100% across men and women for the 'mainly self' category.

7. Resident carers - conclusions

This report using 1991 BHPS data suggests that the prevalence of informal care and the patterns of carers' characteristics in Britain have not undergone any significant changes during the period from 1985 to 1991, as determined by 1985 GHS data. One in seven adults aged over 16 were providing informal care for someone either inside or outside their own household and a fifth of all households contained at least one carer. These proportions are virtually identical to those observed in the 1985 GHS data. One of the noticeable differences observed between the 1991 and 1985 figures was that a greater proportion of persons over the age of 65 are caring for someone inside their own household. Furthermore, the 1991 data suggests that the proportion of individuals over the age of 75 who are carers is high, particularly for men.

The co-resident carers identified in this report were predominantly in the older age groups, with over 30% being of retirement age, whereas half of those caring for a sick, disabled or elderly person outside the household fell into the 45-65 age band. The younger group of carers generally had characteristics which parallel those of the general population.

Recent research tells us that women are more often than not the main carer of a dependant inside the household, and that many of Britain's carers have to juggle the tasks of caring and paid employment (Arber and Ginn 1991; Victor 1991). Our survey suggests that caring is not an exclusively female task, but that there was an equal proportion of men in the population caring for a co-resident. However, the BHPS data did find that those spending long hours caring for co-residents continue to be women who are looking after the home.

Caring time is clearly related to the degree of disability of the dependant. Although the Wave 1 BHPS data did not permit this aspect of caring to be examined, it did look at the distribution of time spent caring for different types of care recipient, in terms of the relationship to the carer.

Many carers were themselves elderly and caring for an elderly spouse, including a significant number of men. These results do not conform to the traditional stereotype of carers being female and middle-aged. According to demographic projections the need for caring is likely to increase in the foreseeable future. Furthermore, it is anticipated that the burden of caring for a very elderly parent will fall disproportionately on daughters and daughters-in-law (Hantrais et al 1990). We observed a greater proportion of individuals looking after parents than the 1985 figures suggested; further, these statistics probably underestimate this phenomenon because parents-in-law were not included in the analysis for co-resident carers.

Carers may have to forego employment opportunities or change their working patterns to fit around their caring obligations. The BHPS data revealed that 9% of women co-resident carers had had to give up their jobs to care. This supports earlier existing findings suggesting the situation is unchanged (Jones and Vetter, 1984). Furthermore, of those looking after sick or disabled children, we detected a disproportionate number of mothers looking after the home and fathers who were unemployed, compared to the general population. This supports other studies reporting that both mothers and fathers of physically disabled children are less likely to be in paid employment than other parents (Smythe and Robus 1989). Where disability in adult life is concerned the majority of care is provided by spouses. A study by Martin and White (1988) suggested that male spouse carers were less likely to be in paid employment than female spouse carers. Although our data do not support this finding, we found significantly fewer male co-resident carers of working age in employment compared to the male population of working age.

The financial situation of caring households in the BHPS was generally found to be poorer than that of the general population, with household income clustering in the lowest and second quintiles of the distribution. A similar picture of a poorer standard of living for carers and their households has been observed in other studies (Arber and Ginn 1992; Martin and White 1988). The distribution of occupations and social class of carers in employment further confirms other studies which have found a clear class gradient based on occupation, for the probability of being a carer. This is seen typically for both men and women, and particularly for those under the age of 44 (Arber and Ginn 1992). BHPS data confirms that a disproportionate number of co-resident carers were in the manual occupations with twice as many in unskilled manual jobs. Extra-resident carers, on the other hand, tended to have a broadly parallel occupational distribution to all employees, but with a greater number in managerial or technical jobs.

The BHPS has an advantage over other large scale data sets in that it contains a set of questions on the organisation of household finances and domestic tasks. These measures suggest that partners in co-resident carers' households were less likely to share responsibilities for such tasks than couples in general, but that male carers described themselves as taking on a greater share of these duties than all men. The attitudes held by carers towards women's work and the family were, for male co-resident carers, more traditional than men as a whole, whilst their female counterparts tended to be more liberal on some issues but less so on others, than all women. These findings, in part, are certainly likely to reflect the age of carers, with older groups holding less egalitarian or feminist views.

Patterns of informal care in the community may be expected to undergo fairly radical changes in the forthcoming years. The timing of this report coincides with the April 1993 first stage of the implementation of the NHS Care and Community Act (DH 1989). Other authors foresee far reaching changes in the financing and organisation of community and residential care (Laczko and Victor 1992). The responsibility will fall on Local Authorities to assess the 'package of care' required for a disabled, sick or elderly person. This will necessarily involve carers who may be required to take a greater involvement in negotiating the most suitable package for their dependant. Moreover, the privatisation of care and the selling of services required by many care recipients may place a greater burden on family members and relatives who cannot afford to pay for these services.

The BHPS longitudinal dataset will provide a very suitable vehicle for examining the consequences of this act. Because we are following the present 1991 sample of individual carers and care recipients over time, we can readily assess changes in the lives of these individuals and households.

SECTION B
CHILD CARERS

8. Childcare responsibilities and employment

In this part of the caring report responsibilities for dependent children are examined. Previous studies examining childcare in relation to women's employment have highlighted the limited availability and use of formal childcare facilities such as day nurseries in Britain. In addition the widespread use of informal types of care provided by relatives and friends free of charge has also been noted (see Martin and Roberts, 1984; Dex, 1986; Cohen, 1990). The cost of childcare which may act as a disincentive to take on paid employment where expected earnings are relatively low has also been addressed (see for example Dex, 1986). Childbearing and childrearing clearly have considerable implications for women's employment participation and earnings potential as it is women who in general continue to be regarded as primarily responsible for the care of children. In Section 8 the characteristics of all households and individuals with dependent children are examined. Sections 9 and 10 examine the use and cost of childcare facilities for respondents in employment with childcare responsibilities for children aged twelve years or under. The use and cost of childcare facilities are related to the numbers and ages of children, who cares for children when they are ill, parents' occupations, hours of work, individual and household income and attitudes to women's employment and women's roles within the family. The analysis enables the types of strategies adopted by individuals and households for combining childcare responsibilities and employment to begin to be addressed.

Characteristics of households with dependent children

Of the 5511 households in the BHPS (1991) sample 31% (n=1707) had at least one dependent child under the age of 16 present. When we apply a definition of dependent child which includes children up to the age of 18 if they are still in full-time education 33% (n=1820) of households had at least one dependent child present. These compare with the estimates in the 1991 GHS (1993, HMSO, p.24) where 30% of households had dependent children present[1]. The main focus of this report is the way in which the care of young children and the employment of parents interact. The analysis therefore defines 'dependent children' as those aged under 16 years. In addition only respondents of working age i.e. men aged under 64 years and women aged under 60 years are included in the analysis[2]. Table 8.1 sets out the total number of households in the BHPS 1991 sample by the number of dependent children according to both definitions of dependent children[3].

Table 8.1   BHPS 1991: Households with dependent children aged under 16 and under 18 in full-time education.

	Number of households			
	Aged < 16		Aged < 18	
	Freq	%	Freq	%
Number of children				
None	3804	69	3691	67
One	709	13	714	13
Two	692	13	767	14
Three	235	4	259	5
Four	59	1	65	1
Five and over	12	—	15	—
Total	5511	100	5511	100

The 1707 households with at least one dependent child aged under 16 years will therefore form the sub-sample for the analysis. Within these households 2837 parents[4] completed a full individual interview. It should be noted that in the case of couple households it was not always possible to interview both parents. In 176 cases only one member of the married or cohabiting couple was interviewed. The number of respondents from couple households where both parents were interviewed was 2404. Of the 2837 parents interviewed 91% (n=2580) were members of a married or cohabiting couple and 9% (n=257) of parents interviewed were lone parents[5]. At the household level a total of 16% (n=277) of households with a dependent under 16 years were headed by a lone parent. This compares with the 1991 GHS (ibid) where 19% of households with dependent children (<16 or 16-18 if in full-time education) were headed by a lone parent.

Table 8.2 gives the distribution of age, marital status, age of the youngest child in the household and monthly household income for those with dependent children by the number of dependent children under 16 years. In total 82% (n=2319) of those with dependent children were aged between 26 and 45 years. As could be expected those aged between 16 and 25 years and at the beginning of their child-rearing years were more likely than older groups to have only one dependent child. The majority of respondents with dependent children under 16 years were married, with 84% (n=2388) being married, 6% (n=165) cohabiting, 3% (83) single, 1% (n=23) widowed, 4% (n=108) divorced and 2% (n=71) separated[6]. The gross mean monthly household income for households with dependent children under 16 was £1872 per month[7]. There was little difference in the gross mean monthly household income according to family size. For households with one dependent child the mean was £1998, for those with two children £1778, for those with three children £1744 and for those with four or more £2005. In addition the number of dependent children were distributed similarly across each income group. Between 37% and 45% of each income group had one dependent child and 38% to 45% had two dependent children.

Employment activity and employment characteristics

Figure 1 gives the distribution of current employment activity by the age of the youngest child. Of the 2837 respondents with dependent children under 16 years 72% (n=2041) were in paid

employment and 28% (n=796) were not in current paid employment. Of those in paid employment 55% (n=1117) were men and 45% (n=924) were women. In addition 6% (n=122) of those in paid employment were lone parents. The majority, 92% (n=112) of these working lone parents were women. Of the 2041 respondents in paid employment 13% (n=261) were working under 16 hours per week, 15% (n=315) between 16 and 29 hours per week while 69% (n=1417) were working 30 hours or more per week[8]. If we look at the hours worked by female lone parents 56% (n=63) were working 30 hours or more per week, 20% (n=22) worked between 16 and 29 hours per week while 24% (n=27) worked under 16 hours per week. As discussed later in the report there may be a tendency for lone parents to work full-time[9] if they do not have access to free or inexpensive childcare. Gender also affects the number of hours worked with the overwhelming majority of those working under 30 hours per week being women and the majority of full-time workers being men.

Of the 796 respondents not in current employment 26% (n=204) were unemployed[10] and 74% (n=593) were economically inactive. In the BHPS survey respondents who were economically inactive were asked if they would like some regular paid employment even if only for a few hours per week. Of those who were economically inactive 56% (n=329) said they would like some regular paid employment while 44% (n=263) said they would not like any paid employment.

Table 8.2   BHPS 1991: Characteristics of respondents with dependent children aged under 16 years by number of children present.

	Number of children				Frequency	Total
---	One	Two	Three	Four +		col %
			row %			
Age*						
16-25	53	39	6	9	244	9
26-35	32	45	17	6	1187	42
36-45	41	41	15	3	1132	40
46-59	69	25	4	2	270	9
Marital status						
Married	39	43	15	4	2388	84
Cohabiting	52	38	8	2	165	6
Single	65	22	13	—	83	3
Widowed	43	32	15	10	23	1
Divorced	52	36	6	6	108	4
Separated	47	31	14	8	70	2
Age of youngest child						
Under 2 years	38	42	15	5	948	33
3 - 4 years	25	44	24	7	360	13
5 - 11 years	29	50	18	3	987	35
12 - 15 years	79	21	—	—	519	18
Missing					24	1
Gross monthly h'hold income*						
Under £500	45	38	15	2	135	6
£501-£1000	40	38	16	6	393	18
£1001-£1500	37	45	11	7	455	20
£1501-£2000	38	43	15	4	478	22
£2001-£3000	43	41	14	1	503	23
Over £3000	44	42	10	5	249	11
Total	1163	1167	399	108	2837	100

*   Note 4 cases of a parent between 60-64 not included.

**   Marital status as reported by respondents.

*** Gross monthly household income includes all labour and non-labour
     income in the month before interview.
     Monthly household income not available in 624 cases.

Figure 1 **BHPS 1991: Current employment activity of those with dependent children under 16 years by age of youngest child.**

All child<16

n=2837   100%

45%	Men
55%	Women
47%	Child <5
35%	Child 5-11
18%	Child 12-15

In paid employment

n=2041   72%

55%	Men
45%	Women
39%	Child <5
39%	Child 5-11
22%	Child 12-15

Not in paid employment

n=796   28%

22%	Men
78%	Women
65%	Child <5
25%	Child 5-11
10%	Child 12-15

<16 hrs per wk

n=261   13%

3%	Men
97%	Women
42%	Child <5
43%	Child 5-11
15%	Child 12-15

16-29 hrs per wk

n=315   15%

5%	Men
95%	Women
30%	Child <5
46%	Child 5-11
24%	Child 12-15

30+ hrs per wk

n=1417   69%

75%	Men
25%	Women
41%	Child <5
37%	Child 5-11
22%	Child 12-15

Unemployed

n=204   26%

57%	Men
43%	Women
61%	Child <5
29%	Child 5-11
10%	Child 12-15

Inactive

n=592   74%

10%	Men
90%	Women
66%	Child <5
24%	Child 5-11
10%	Child 12-15

*   missing information on hours in 2% (n=48) cases.*

Wants job

n=329   56%

10%	Men
90%	Women
66%	Child <5
26%	Child 5-11
8%	Child 12-15

Not want job

n=263   44%

9%	Men
91%	Women
66%	Child <5
21%	Child 5-11
13%	Child 12-15

It is interesting to note that the presence of a child under the age of five does not deter some of the inactive from wanting a paid job. Of those wanting some regular employment 66% had a child under five years. Although childcare responsibilities for young children may constrain some women to withdraw from paid employment they may still want regular paid employment. The percentage of the inactive wanting a job who had young children under five years was almost the same as the percentage of those with older children wanting employment. Overall 56% (=217) of the inactive with young children wanted a job compared to 55% (n=111) of those with older children.

As previous research has demonstrated the presence of dependent children is particularly important in understanding women's movements into and out of the labour market over time (see for example Martin and Roberts, 1984; Dex, 1987; Joshi, 1989). When we compare the distributions of current employment activity for men and women by the age of the youngest child the BHPS data confirm other research in this area. Table 8.3 sets out the distribution of current employment activity by age of youngest child and gender. Men were more likely to be in full-time paid employment regardless of the age of the youngest child. Men with children aged two years or under were more likely to be unemployed but this is possibly due to an age effect with younger men being more likely to be unemployed. There is no evidence that men are reducing their hours of employment when young children are present. For women there is also a clear pattern with women being less likely than men to be in full-time employment regardless of the age of the youngest child. However women with a youngest child aged over eleven were more likely than women with children under eleven to be in full-time employment. In addition 53% (n=276) of women with a child two years or under were economically inactive as were 42% (n=83) of those with a youngest child aged between three and four. The percentage of economically inactive women falls to 23% (n=124) once the youngest child reaches school-age. But of the 539 women with children aged between five and eleven years, only 24% (n=131) were in full-time employment while 46% (n=245) worked fewer than 30 hours per week. In general the pattern of women with pre-school age children withdrawing from paid employment and returning to primarily part-time employment once children reach school-age is confirmed in the BHPS data. But there is evidence to suggest that some women are maintaining a presence in the labour market during the early child-rearing years. Overall 41% of women with a youngest child two years or under and 47% of

women with a youngest child aged between three and four were in paid employment, albeit mainly part-time. Only between 14% and 15% of those with pre-school age children were working full-time with part-time employment being undertaken by most of these women.

Table 8.4 gives the occupations, employment status, contractual status and monthly gross pay of respondents in employment by gender. As can be seen from the table men were more likely to be in managerial, administrative or professional occupations than women while women were more likely to be in personal service or sales occupations. Men were more likely to be self-employed when compared to women. Women were more likely to be in seasonal or temporary jobs than men. The differences on usual monthly gross pay are also marked with 98% (n=171) of those earning up to £200 per month and 89% (n=402) of those earning between £201 and £700 per month being women. In contrast 81% (n=266) of those earning between £1001 and £1500 per month and 83% (n=167) of those earning between £1501 and £2000 per month were men.

Table 8.5 crosstabulates occupation and usual gross pay by usual hours worked and gender. Of the 252 women working under sixteen hours per week only 16% (n=50) were in professional occupations, 18% (n=46) were in clerical or secretarial occupations and 66% (n=166) were in personal service, sales, plant operatives or other occupations. Women working between 16 and 29 hours per week were most likely to be in clerical/craft or personal service/sales occupations with 63% (n=187) being in these categories. As previously noted women with children were more likely to be in part-time employment and less likely to be in professional occupations than men. However, of women with dependent children under sixteen who were in full-time employment 42% (n=147) had professional occupations. When we examine usual monthly gross pay by usual weekly hours worked and gender, women with dependent children who were working full-time earned significantly less than men with dependent children who were in full-time employment. Of women working 30 hours or more per week 42% (n=119) had usual monthly earnings of between £201 and £700 compared to only 6% (n=49) of men in full-time employment. In addition, only 13% (n=37) of women working full-time had usual earnings over £1500 per month compared to 40% (n=303) of men in full-time employment.

Combining childcare responsibilities with paid employment may lead two parent families to adopt strategies of working at differing times of day so that one parent is always available to care for children while the other is working. Table 8.6 sets out the times of day worked and the preference for numbers of hours worked by gender. Overall 51% (n=1032) of respondents said they worked during the day. However, 90% (n=138) of those working mornings or afternoons only were women as were 79% (n=124) of those working evenings or nights only. This suggests that some women with childcare responsibilities arrange their working hours to coincide with the school day or when their spouse or other family members are available to care for children in the evening. When asked whether they would like to work fewer hours, more hours or

continue with the same hours 48% (n=990) of respondents said they would like to continue with the same hours but this varies according to gender. Overall women appeared to be more content with their current hours than men. Of the women, 57% (n=523) wanted to continue working the same hours compared to 42% (n=467) of men. Men were also more likely than women to want to work fewer hours per week while women were more likely to want to work more hours. Thirty two percent (n=353) of men wanted to work fewer hours compared to 21% (n=193) of women while only 5% (n=55) of men wanted to work more hours compared to 12% (n=111) of women.

Table 8.3   BHPS 1991: Current employment activity by age of youngest child and gender

| | Age of youngest child | | | | | | | |
| | 0 - 2 | | 3 - 4 | | 5 - 11 | | 12 - 15 | |
	Men	Women	Men	Women	Men	Wo men	Men	Women
Current activity								
	%	%	%	%	%	%	%	%
Employed	**82**	**41**	**87**	**47**	**90**	**71**	**8 8**	**81**
Under 16 hours	(.5)	13	—	20	1	20	1	13
16 - 29 hours	1	12	—	13	1	26	1	25
30 hours and over	78	15	87	14	86	24	83	41
(Missing hours)	2	1	—	—	2	1	3	2
Not employed	**18**	**59**	**13**	**53**	**10**	**29**	**1 2**	**19**
Unemployed	14	6	8	11	6	6	7	2
Inactive	4	53	5	42	4	23	5	17
Base = 100%	431	517	160	200	448	539	241	278

Base: All = 2813, Men = 1279, Women 1534

24 cases with missing information excluded.

48

Table 8.4   BHPS 1991: Employment characteristics of respondents in employment with dependent children aged under sixteen by gender

	Men row %	Women row %	Freq	Total col %
Occupation **				
Professional/administration	64	36	675	33
Clerical/craft	57	43	592	29
Service/sales	31	69	360	20
Plant/other	58	42	407	20
Missing	—	—	7	—
Total			2041	100
Employment status**				
Employee	52	48	1729	85
Self-employed	73	27	312	15
Total			2011	100
Contractual status**				
Permanent job	57	43	1841	90
Seasonal/temporary	17	83	106	5
Contract/fixed period	54	46	90	4
Missing	—	—	4	—
Total			2041	100
Monthly gross pay**				
Under £200	(2)	98	175	11
£201 - £700	11	89	455	29
£701 - £1000	64	36	252	16
£1001 - £1500	81	19	330	21
£1501 - £2000	83	17	200	10
Over £2000	97	(3)	153	10
Total			1565	100

**   sig < .001

Brackets denote cell sizes under ten cases

Usual monthly gross pay not available in 476 cases

Table 8.5 **BHPS 1991: Occupation and usual monthly gross pay by usual hours worked per week and gender**

	Usual hours worked per week					
	< 16		16 - 29		30+	
	Men	Women**	Men	Women**	Men	Women**
	%	%	%	%	%	%
Occupation						
Professional/administration	21	16	35	17	38	42
Clerical/craft	8	18	30	33	31	30
Service/sales	35	39	18	30	10	17
Plant/other	36	27	17	20	21	11
Base = 100%	9	252	14	298	1065	350
Monthly gross pay						
Up to £200	(55)	71	—	5	—	(1)
£201 - £700	(22)	28	(13)	85	6	42
£701 - £1000	—	(1)	(39)	8	20	24
£1001 - £1500	—	—	(13)	(2)	34	20
£1501 - £2000	(23)	—	(35)	—	21	11
Over £2000	—	—	—	—	19	2
Base = 100%	5	211	8	261	772	286

*** sig < .001*

Base: All = 1988, Men = 1087, Women = 901

53 cases with missing information excluded, monthly gross pay missing in 476 cases.

Brackets denote cell sizes under ten cases

Household employment types

The trend for women to return to paid employment during their child-rearing years has led to a growing interest in dual-earner households, in particular whether there is anything distinctive about dual-earner households when compared to sole-earner households (see for example Brannen and Moss, 1987). In addition the growth of lone parent families has produced a number of questions regarding equality of access to paid employment for those who are solely responsible for the care of young children. The BHPS data allow us to categorise households (Table 8.7) and individual respondents (Table 8.8) with dependent children into household employment types according to the employment status of the parent(s) and the age of the youngest child. As Table 8.7 shows 45% (n=763) of households with children under 16 were dual-earner couple households, 28% (n=478) sole-earner couple households, 16% (n=277) were lone parent households and 8% (n=138) were no-earner couples. In Table 8.8, 51% (n=1438) of interviewed respondents with dependent children under 16 years were members of dual-earner households, 30% (n=851) in sole-earner households, 9% (n=257) were lone parents, half of whom were in paid employment, and 8% (n=225) were in households where neither parent was in employment.

Table 8.9 gives the number of dependent children in the household according to the household employment type with the most marked differences being between those in dual-earner and sole-earner couples with a youngest child aged between 5 and 15 years. Of those with one child, 38% (n=423) were members of a dual-earner couple with a child aged between 5 and fifteen years while 13% (n=146) were

Table 8.6 **BHPS 1991: Times of day worked and preference for hours worked for respondents with dependent children aged under sixteen by gender**

	Men[a] row %	Women[b] row %	Men[a] Col %	Women[b] Col %	All[c] Freq	Total Col %
**Times of day worked **						
Morning/afternoon only	10	90	1	15	153	7
During day	59	41	54	46	1032	51
Evening/night only	21	79	3	13	158	8
Shift/other times	68	32	13	7	215	11
Varies	52	48	8	9	167	8
Missing/NA	72	28	21	9	316	15
**Preferred hours **						
Work fewer hours	65	35	32	21	546	27
Work more hours	33	67	5	12	167	8
Work same hours	47	53	42	57	990	48
Missing/NA	71	29	22	11	339	17

** sig < 0.001

[a] Base 100% Men = 1117

[b] Base 100% Women = 924

[c] Base 100% All = 2041

in a sole-earner couple with a child between 5 and 15. Where two children were present 35% (n=403) of respondents were in a dual-earner couple and 11% (n=129) in a sole-earner couple with a child aged between 5 and 15 years. In addition the data indicate that as the number of children increases the probability of being a sole-earner household also increases. Where there is more than one child and the youngest is aged under five, the family is more likely to have only one earner, probably due to the woman's withdrawal from paid employment.

Table 8.10 shows the gross mean monthly household income[11] for all households with dependent children was £1872. Dual-earner households had the highest mean monthly income at £2393 per month. The age of the youngest child did however affect the mean income level. Dual-earner households with a youngest child under five years had a mean monthly income of £2011 and those with children between 5 and 15 years a mean monthly income of £2600. This is possibly due to the tendency for women to increase the numbers of hours they work once children reach school age (see Table 8.3). For sole-earner couples the age of the youngest child does not

have any marked effect on the mean monthly household income of £1692. Lone parents had a mean monthly income of £806. However there was a wide variation depending on the employment status of the parent. Lone parents not in current employment with a youngest child aged under five years had the lowest mean monthly income at £526 while those with children between 5 and 15 years had a mean monthly income only slightly higher at £573. Lone parents with a youngest child aged under five who were in employment had a mean monthly income of £1068, increasing slightly to £1117 for lone parents with children aged between 5 and 15 years. Couples where neither partner was in employment had a mean monthly household income at £781. One could argue that no-earner couples with dependent children have the lowest household income worked out on an adult per capita basis while for lone parents, access to paid employment is clearly critical.

Table 8.7   BHPS 1991: Household employment types for households with dependent children < 16.

	Freq		%	
Dual-earner couple	763		45	
Child < 5		266		16
Child 5 - 15		497		29
Sole-earner couple	478		28	
Child < 5		286		17
Child 5 - 15		192		11
Lone parent	277		16	
In employment/child <5		32		2
In employment/child 5 - 15		106		6
Not employed/child <5		81		5
Not employed/child 5 - 15		58		3
No-earner* couple	138		8	
Child < 16				
Other**	40		2	
Total***	1697		100	

*   *'No-earner' includes both unemployed and economically inactive.*

**   *'Other' includes lone parents living within families and multi-couple households.*

***   *Total n differs as 10 households unable to be classified due to missing information.*

Table 8.8   BHPS 1991: Household employment types for respondents with dependent children < 16.

	Freq		%	
Dual-earner couples	1438		51	
Child < 5		495		18
Child 5 - 15		943		33
Sole-earner couples	851		30	
Child < 5		524		19
Child 5 - 15		327		11
Lone parents	257		9	
In employment/child <5		29		1
In employment/child 5 - 15		101		3
Not employed/child <5		76		3
Not employed/child 5 - 15		52		2
No-earner* couples	226		8	
Child < 16				
Other**	66		2	
Total	2873	100		

*   *'No-earner' includes both unemployed and economically inactive.*

**   *'Other' includes lone parents living within families and multi-couple households.*

Table 8.9   BHPS 1991: Household employment type by number of dependent children under16

	Number of children			
	One	Two	Three	Four+
	%	%	%	%
Dual-earner couples				
Child <5	17	17	21	15
Child 5 - 15	38	35	25	16
Sole-earner couples				
Child <5	14	21	23	26
Child 5 - 15	13	11	12	(5)
Lone parents				
In employment/child <5	2	(.5)	(.1)	(1)
In employment/child 5 - 15	5	3	(1)	(1)
Not employed/child <5	2	2	4	(6)
Not employed/child 5 - 15	2	2	(2)	(5)
No-earner couple				
Child <16	6	8	11	25
Base = 100%	1113	1154	396	108

Base: All = 2771

*   sig < .001*

Brackets denote cell sizes under ten cases

Table 8.10   BHPS 1991: Gross mean monthly household income for household employment types

	Mean monthly household income*
Household type	
Dual-earner couples	**£2393**
Child < 5	£2011
Child 5 - 15	£2600
Sole-earner couples	**£1692**
Child < 5	£1707
Child 5 - 15	£1666
Lone parents	**£806**
In employment/child <5	£1068
In employment/child 5 - 15	£1117
Not employed/child <5	£526
Not employed/child 5 - 15	£573
No-earner couples	
Child < 16	£781
All households	£1872

*   *Gross household income in month before interview.*

Footnotes to Chapter 8

1. The GHS definition of dependent children includes children aged <16 and those aged 16-18 years if in full-time education. No comparable figure for children aged <16 only are available.

2. There were six cases only of parents aged over working age.

3. Weighted data only are reported throughout.

4. A 'parent' may be the natural parent, step or adoptive parent or, if none of these are present, another adult who is reported as being responsible for the child.

5. Lone parents are defined as those with a dependent child(ren) <16 where no spouse was resident within the household at the time of interview.

6. Marital status as reported by respondents. There were some cases where respondents describing themselves as 'married' did not have a spouse living with them in the household. Similarly some reported themselves as 'divorced' or 'separated' even though they had a spouse within the current household.

7. Gross income includes all household income, labour and non-labour, in the month preceding interview. Total household income was not available for 624 cases.

8. Information on usual hours worked missing in 2% (n=48) cases.

9. Full-time employment is defined as working 30 hours or more per week.

10. The unemployed are defined in accordance with the LFS (ILO/OECD) i.e. all those not currently employed who had either looked for work at some time in the last four weeks or were waiting to take up a job already obtained.

11. Gross monthly household income includes all labour and non-labour income in the month before interview.

9. Use of childcare facilities

The availability and cost of childcare are clearly central to women's decision to take on paid employment. As Cohen (1988, 1990) and Moss (1990) have documented, the availability of childcare in the UK is limited as there is no statutory obligation on local authorities to provide childcare except where children are defined as 'in need'. Private nurseries and registered childminders provide a limited amount of care and as no comprehensive childcare service exists it has been suggested that families rely on informal care provided by friends and relatives or arrange their working hours to fit in with childcare responsibilities. These issues are examined in this section.

The BHPS survey included a series of questions regarding the use and cost of childcare facilities where dependent children of twelve years or under were present. Respondents who were in current employment and defined as the 'responsible adult' for children in this age group answered this section. The 'responsible adult' is defined as the mother in the BHPS survey except where the mother[1] is not present. In these few cases the 'responsible adult' is then defined by the respondent(s) in the household. It should be stressed that the term 'responsible adult' does not carry any substantive meaning but is used in the survey as a device to gain information on childcare arrangements for those in employment in the most efficient and reliable manner. As women tend to be the ones responsible for childcare arrangements and the main theoretical and policy questions related to childcare issues are concerned with women's employment, asking currently employed women for details of childcare usage was seen as the most reliable means of collecting this information.

A total of 772 respondents answered the section on childcare usage, the vast majority of whom, 98% (n=759), were women. Only thirteen men were defined as the responsible adult for a child of twelve years or under. In 28% (n=214) of cases the youngest child was aged two years or under, in 12% (n=96) between three and four years and in 59% (n=455) between five and twelve years of age. Table 9.1 gives the distribution of numbers of children by the age of the youngest child. In the majority of cases two children were present with 41% (n=87) of those with a youngest child two years or under being in this category and 51% (232) of those with a youngest child between five and twelve years also having another child.

Table 9.2 sets out the characteristics of respondents with dependent children aged twelve years or under by the number of children present. The majority of respondents fell within the 26 - 45 age range (89%) and the majority (83%) were married. There was no significant relationship between monthly household income and the number of children present. Table 9.3 gives the occupations of respondents with childcare responsibilities for children aged twelve or under. Respondents were fairly evenly spread across occupations with 27% (n=205) being in professional/ administrative occupations, 28% (n=12) in clerical or craft occupations, 26% (n=207) in personal service or sales occupations and 19% (n=147) in other occupations.

Table 9.1   BHPS 1991: Number of dependent children under 16 by age of youngest child

| Number of children | Age of youngest | | | | | |
| | 0 - 2 | | 3 - 4 | | 5 - 12 | |
	Freq	%	Freq	%	Freq	%
One	96	45	28	29	154	34
Two	87	41	39	40	232	51
Three or more	31	14	29	30	69	15
Total	214	100	96	100	455	100

Base n=765

n differs as missing information in 7 cases.

Table 9.2 BHPS 1991: Characteristics of respondents with dependent children aged twelve or under by number of children present

	One	Two	Number of children Three row %	Four+	Freq	Total col %
Age**						
16 - 25	53	43	2	—	50	6
26 - 35	36	45	16	4	386	50
36 - 45	32	51	15	2	303	39
46 - 59	62	32	6	—	33	4
					772	100
Marital status*						
Married	33	49	16	3	639	83
Cohabiting	52	41	(5)	(2)	39	5
Single	75	(6)	(19)	—	22	3
Widowed	(29)	(58)	(13)	—	6	1
Divorced	49	40	(7)	(4)	41	5
Separated	49	44	(4)	(3)	25	3
					772	100
Number in household**						
Two	100	—	—	—	35	4
Three	87	13	—	—	218	29
Four	11	87	(2)	—	331	43
Five or more	9	23	56	11	182	24
Missing	—	—	—	—	6	—
					772	100
Monthly household income						
Under £500	(52)	(29)	(20)	—	14	2
£501 - £1000	39	45	(12)	(4)	75	13
£1001 - £1500	36	50	10	(4)	117	20
£1501 - £2000	36	44	16	(4)	145	25
£2001 - £3000	37	47	15	(1)	161	28
Over £3000	28	59	(9)	(5)	68	12
					580	100

*   sig < .01

**   sig < .001

Brackets denote cell sizes under ten cases.

Monthly household income missing in 192 cases.

Table 9.3   BHPS 1991: Distribution of occupations for respondents with childcare responsibilities for children aged twelve or under

	Frequency		%	
Occupation				
Admin/professional	**205**		**27**	
Manager/administration		43		6
Professional		67		9
Associate professional		95		12
Clerical/craft	**212**		**28**	
Clerical/secretarial		190		25
Craft		22		3
Service/sales	**207**		**26**	
Personal service		127		16
Sales		80		10
Other	**145**		**19**	
Plant operatives		40		5
Other		105		14
Missing	2		—	
Total	772		100	

Respondents were asked to mention up to three types of childcare they used while they were working. Table 9.4 sets out the distribution of the types of childcare used[2]. On the first type of childcare mentioned 61% (n=470) gave a home-based form of childcare, that is they worked while their children were at school, their children looked after themselves until they got home from work, they worked at or from home or their spouse or partner looked after them. In 13% (n=97) of cases an external/formal type of childcare was given as the first type such as having a nanny/mother's help, using a workplace nursery, a day nursery or a childminder. In 22% (n=175) of cases an external/ informal type was given as the first type of care. In these cases a friend or relative or some other form of childcare was used. It is also worth noting that the use of workplace nurseries was negligible, with fewer than 1% of those using an external/formal type giving this type of care.

Of the 742 respondents reporting childcare arrangements 65% (n=481) reported using one type only, 29% (n=214) reported using two types and only 6% (n=47) reported using three types. Table 9.5 shows that the use of one type of childcare was the most common regardless of the number of children and there was no significant relationship between the number of children or the age of the youngest child with the number of types of care used. However the age of the youngest child is significantly related to the type of childcare used for children under three years; for this group the external/formal type of care was most common (see Table 9.6). On the type of care mentioned first 29% (n=61) of respondents with children aged two years or under used an external/formal type of care compared with only 4% (n=19) of those with a youngest child aged between 5 and 12 years. Those with children aged between 5 and 12 years were also most likely to use a home-based form of care with 75% (n=324) mentioning this type of care first. Arranging childcare so that children could be cared for within the home either by the respondent or their partner was the type most often used; care provided by a relative or friend being the next most often mentioned. However, the BHPS data do not provide information on the preferences parents have for

Table 9.4   BHPS 1991: Types of childcare used for dependent children aged 12 or under.

Type of care	1st type Freq	1st type %	2nd type Freq	2nd type %	3rd type Freq	3rd type %
			Order in which care mentioned			
Home-based	**470**	**61**	**83**	**11**	**8**	**1**
Work while at school	219	28	12	2	1	(.1)
Look after themselves	28	4	13	2	—	—
I work from home	47	6	3	—	2	(.3)
Spouse/partner cares	176	23	55	77	5	(.7)
External/formal	**97**	**13**	**30**	**4**	**5**	**1**
Nanny/mothers help	12	2	1	—	1	(.1)
Workplace nursery	3	—	1	—	—	—
Day nursery	27	4	12	2	—	—
Childminder	55	7	16	2	4	(.5)
External/informal	**175**	**22**	**148**	**19**	**34**	**4**
A relative cares	124	16	84	11	17	2
Friend/neighbour cares	25	3	41	5	12	1
Other	26	3	23	3	5	(.7)
Not mentioned	—	—	481	62	695	90
Missing	30	4	30	4	30	4
Total	772	100	772	100	772	100

Brackets denote cell sizes under ten cases.

Table 9.5   BHPS 1991: Number of dependent children and age of youngest child by number of types of childcare used for children aged 12 years or under.

	Number of types of care used One	Two row %	Three	Freq	Total col %
Number of children					
One	68	26	6	263	35
Two	62	31	7	348	47
Three	69	25	(6)	110	15
Four or more	(45)	50	(6)	20	3
Total				741	100
Age of youngest child					
Under 2 years	70	23	7	208	28
3 -4 years	63	30	7	95	13
5 - 12 years	62	31	6	434	59
Missing	—	—	—	4	—
Total				741	100

31 cases with missing information excluded.

differing types of childcare. It may be the case that parents prefer to arrange their working hours to fit in with domestic responsibilities but it may also be the case that this is done as a result of the availability of care or the cost of paid childcare relative to the wages they could expect to earn in the local labour market. The use of relatives as carers is also common and again we would need to consider whether the use of a relative or friend is due to preference, availability, cost or a combination of these factors.

Tables 9.7 to 9.9 give the employment characteristics of respondents responsible for children aged twelve or under by the type of childcare being used[3]. As Table 9.7 shows occupation is significantly related to the first type of care mentioned only. This suggests that the first mentioned type of care is probably the main type of care used in the majority of cases. Of the 97 respondents using an external/formal type of care as the first reported type 53% (n=53) were in professional occupations, 32% (n=31) in clerical or craft occupations and 15% (n=15) in personal service, sales or other occupations. Of the 468 respondents using a home-based form of care 21% (n=98) were in professional occupations, 26% (n=122) were in clerical or craft occupations, 31% (n=144) were in

personal service or sales occupations and 22% (n=104) in other occupations. It is interesting to note that the 174 respondents using an external/informal type of care were evenly spread across occupations. Table 9.8 shows gross monthly earnings and gross monthly household income by the type of care used. As might be expected the type of childcare used was related to level of earnings with the lower earners being more likely to use a home-based type of care and higher earners being more likely to use external/formal types of care. The level of monthly household income is also related to the type of care used although the variations across types of care are much greater between the earnings levels of the 'responsible adult' than they are across household income levels.

Usual weekly hours of work, the times of day worked and the preferences for number of hours worked are all significantly related to the type of childcare mentioned first (see Table 9.9). In total 63% (n=468) of respondents worked fewer than 30 hours per week, with half of these working under 16 hours per week. Of the 222 respondents working under 16 hours per week 80% (n=179) used a home-based form of care while 46% (n=118) of the 256 respondents working 30 or more hours per week used a home-based form of care. However those working 30 hours or more were also most likely to report using an external/informal type of care with 29% (n=74) using this type compared to 16% (n=36) of those working under 16 hours per week. Respondents working during the evening or night were most likely to say they used a home-based form of care. This again suggests that some women are arranging their working times to fit in with the working hours of their partner or spouse who then cares for the children while they are at work. On preferences for the numbers of hours worked 44% (n=66) of those wanting fewer hours used home-based care, 23% (n=35) used an external/formal type of care and 33% (n=49) used an external/informal type of care. Of those wanting to work more hours 71% (n=70) used a home-based types of care, 7% (n=7) an external/formal type, and 22% (n=21) an external/informal type of care. This suggests that the availability of home-based care may enable some women with dependent children to participate in the labour market who otherwise would not do so. Where an external/formal type of care is used there may be less of an incentive to take on extra hours of paid employment unless the expected renumeration is sufficient to cover the additional childcare costs entailed. However it could also be argued that where there is no alternative type of childcare available to women the use of a home-based type of care is in many respects a forced choice. Women

Table 9.6 BHPS 1991: Type of childcare used by age of youngest child

	Age of youngest child		
	0 - 2	3 - 4	5 - 12
	%	%	%
Type of care			
1st mention**			
Home-based	42	62	75
External/formal	29	16	4
External/informal	29	22	21
Base = 100%	208	85	434
2nd mention*			
Home-based	8	10	13
External/formal	8	6	2
External/informal	14	21	22
Not mentioned	70	63	63
Base = 100%	208	85	434

*   sig < .01

**   sig < .001

Base: All = 741, 31 cases with missing information excluded.

relying on home-based types of care may be limited by the lack of alternative childcare facilities and be working fewer hours than they would like.

Clearly the number of hours currently worked in conjunction with the type of childcare used might be expected to influence women's preferences for hours of work. If we control for the number of hours worked there are no statistically significant relationships between preferences for hours worked and the type of care used for women working under 30 hours per week. For women working 30 hours or more some differences do emerge. In total 43% (n–110) of women working full-time wanted to work fewer hours, 1%(n=4) wanted to work more hours, 43% (n=111) wanted to continue with the same hours and 12% (n=30) said the question did not apply to their situation. Those using an external type of care, either formal or informal, were more likely than those using a home-based type of care to say they would prefer to work fewer hours. Of those using an external/formal type of care, 53% (n=34) wanted fewer hours and 54% 9n=40) of those using an external/informal type said the same; this compared to 30% (n=36) of those using home-based types of childcare. Those using a home-based type of care were also more likely to say they wanted to continue working the same hours than women using other types of care. Nearly half, 48% (n=56) of women using a home-based type of care preferred their current hours; this compared to 39% (n=25) of those using an external/formal type and 40% (n=29) of those using an external/informal type. It is difficult

to disentangle the most important factors influencing women's preferences for hours worked without carrying out a multi-variate analysis of some kind. The cost of childcare relative to level of earnings is likely to be an important factor determining their preferences, as are women's attitudes to their role within the family, their commitment to paid employment and the sheer practical difficulties of combining home and work roles.

Table 9.10 sets out the types of childcare used by whether the spouse/partner is in employment. On the type of childcare mentioned first 77% (n=253) of dual-earner couples with children aged between five and twelve used a home-based form of care compared to 85% (n=37) of couples where the spouse was not in employment and 55% (n=33) of lone parents. A higher percentage of lone parents with children in this age group also used an external/informal type of care. Lone parents with children under five years were more likely to use an external/formal type of care than either dual-earner or sole-earner couples. A greater percentage of lone parents also used external/informal types of care than either of the other types of couples. The data suggest that the presence of a spouse is more important for determining the type of childcare used than whether the spouse is in employment or not. However, couples where the spouse was not in employment were most likely to use home-based types of care in comparison to either dual-earner couples or lone parent households.

Table 9.7   BHPS 1991: Occupation by type of childcare used

	Types of care used					
	1st type**			2nd type		
	Home-based	Formal	Informal	Home-based	Formal	Informal
	%	%	%	%	%	%
Occupation						
Professional/administration	21	53	27	33	36	26
Clerical/craft	26	32	28	20	43	35
Personal service/sales	31	10	26	29	14	22
Other	22	5	18	18	7	17
Base = 100%	468	97	174	82	30	148

** *sig < .0001*

Base: All = 739, 33 cases with missing information excluded.

Table 9.8   BHPS 1991: Monthly gross earnings and monthly household income by type of childcare used.

| | Type of childcare mentioned first | | | Total | |
| | Home-based | Formal | Informal | | |
		row %		Freq	col %
Monthly gross earnings					
Under £200	79	(1)	20	148	24
£201 - £700	64	10	26	321	52
£701 - £1000	40	32	26	69	11
£1001 - £1500	37	38	25	49	8
Over £1500	31	43	(26)	32	5
Total				619	100
Gross monthly household income*					
Under £500	68	(6)	(26)	14	2
£501 - £1000	61	(9)	30	74	13
£1001 - £1500	71	(7)	22	111	201
£1501 - £2000	64	12	23	142	25
£2001 - £3000	56	16	26	152	27
Over £3000	54	27	19	66	12
Total				560	100

*   sig < .05

**   sig < .0001

Information on monthly gross pay missing in 122 cases.

Information on gross monthly household income missing in 181 cases.

Brackets denote cell sizes under 10 cases.

Attitudes to the family and women's employment

As previously noted one of the difficulties when examining women's employment and childcare issues is disentangling preferences from the availability and cost of childcare. Respondents in the BHPS survey answered a short self-completion questionnaire which included a series of attitudinal questions regarding the role of women within the family and employment. In addition respondents were asked to report who cared for children aged twelve or under when they were ill, providing an indicator of the main carer within the household. On the attitudinal items respondents were asked whether they agreed or disagreed with a series of statements on a five point scale from strongly agree to strongly disagree. The statements used in this analysis were as follows:

A pre-school child is likely to suffer if his or her mother works.

All in all, family life suffers when the woman has a full-time job.

A woman and her family would all be happier if she goes out to work.

Both the husband and wife should contribute to the household income.

Having a full-time job is the best way for a woman to be an independent person.

A husband's job is to earn money; a wife's job is to look after the home and family.

Employers should make special arrangements to help mothers combine jobs and childcare.

A single parent can bring up children as well as a couple

Table 9.9   BHPS 1991: Hours of work, times of day worked and preferences for hours worked by type of childcare used

	Type of childcare mentioned first							
	Home-based[a]	Formal[b]	Formal[c]	Home-base[d]	Formal	Informal	All	
		row %		col %	col %	col %	Freq	col %
Usual weekly hours**								
Under 16	80	3	16	38	8	21	222	30
16 - 29	66	10	25	34	24	35	246	33
30 and over	46	25	29	25	66	42	256	35
DK/missing	(67)	(8)	(25)	(3)	(2)	(2)	18	2
Total							741	100
Times of day worked**								
Mornings/afternoons only	67	(7)	26	16	(8)	17	113	15
During day	53	21	26	37	71	48	326	44
Evenings/nights only	83	(1)	16	20	(1)	11	114	15
Shifts/other times	50	17	33	6	(9)	10	54	8
Varies/NA	75	8	17	21	11	13	133	18
Total							741	100
Preferences for hours worked**								
Want fewer hours	44	23	33	14	36	28	150	20
Want more hours	71	7	22	15	(7)	12	99	13
Continue same hours	66	12	22	59	50	53	419	57
DK/missing/NA	77	(9)	15	12	(6)	6	73	10
Total							741	100

**   *sig < .001*

Brackets denote cell sizes of fewer than 10 cases

a   Base 100% - home based care = 470

b   Base 100% - formal care = 97

c   Base 100% - informal care = 174

Using the total score for all items we can create a four item scale on the attitudinal items from 'traditional' through to 'modern', where 'traditional' represents the lowest quarter of the distribution of scores and 'modern' represents the highest quarter of the distribution[4]. The terminology therefore represents an individual's position within the distribution and should not be interpreted otherwise. In total 64% (n=492) held 'mixed modern' attitudes and 26% (n=205) had 'modern' attitudes. Only one respondent held 'traditional' attitudes and 9% (n=68) 'mixed traditional' attitudes. Perhaps not surprisingly respondents attitudes were concentrated in the 'mixed modern' and 'modern' categories. As these respondents were mainly women in current employment they could be expected to hold positive views on combining employment and raising a family. An age effect is also likely with parents of children under 12 years tending to be younger and possibly more likely to hold less 'traditional' attitudes to women's roles within the family and employment than older respondents.

Table 9.10 BHPS 1991: Type of childcare used by household type

Type of care	Dual-earner		Sole-earner		Lone parent	
	Child <5	Child 5-12	Child <5	Child 5-12	Child <5	Child 5-12
	%	%	%	%	%	%
1st type**						
Home-based	50	77	61	85	11	55
External/formal	24	4	20	—	44	8
External/informal	26	19	19	15	46	37
Base = 100%	240	329	37	44	27	59
2nd type**						
Home-based	9	14	8	16	7	6
External/formal	5	2	18	—	10	5
External/informal	17	26	11	14	17	17
Not mentioned	69	60	62	70	66	72
Base = 100%	240	329	37	44	27	59

** sig < .001

Base: All = 736, 36 cases with missing information excluded.

The type of childcare used might be expected to be influenced by the attitudes held by the parent(s). Table 9.11 gives the type of childcare mentioned first and who looks after children when they are ill by attitudes held to women's role. Of those using a home-based type of care 68% (n=316) had 'mixed modern' attitudes while 20% (n=93) held 'modern' attitudes. Where an external/formal type of care was used 45% (n=44) held 'mixed modern' attitudes and 54% (n=52) 'modern' attitudes. As with those using home-based types of care those using external/informal types of care were more likely to have 'mixed modern' attitudes with 64% (n=110) in this category compared to 34% (n=55) with 'modern' attitudes. If we look at the column percentages a clear pattern is evident with those holding 'mixed traditional' attitudes being least likely to use an external type of childcare either formal or informal. Of those with 'mixed traditional' attitudes 86% (n=55) used a home-based type of care compared to 46% (n=93) of those with 'modern' attitudes. Only one respondent with 'mixed traditional' attitudes used an external/formal type of childcare while 26% (n=52) of those with 'modern' attitudes did so. It might have been expected that those with more

traditional attitudes would prefer a relative or friend to care for their children. However, those with more traditional attitudes were about half as likely as those with more modern attitudes to use an external/informal type of childcare.

Overall women were reported as the main carer of ill children in 66% (n=492) of cases and, of these, 66% (n=330) held 'mixed modern' attitudes. The results did not differ where the man was reported as the main carer; 65% (n=54) of these respondents had 'mixed modern' attitudes and 31% (n=25) had 'modern' attitudes. It is also interesting to note that in 19% (n=143) of cases a person outside the household was reported as the main carer when children were ill rather than the responsible adult or their spouse or partner. As with the type of care used, who looked after ill children was related to the attitudes held. Of those with 'mixed traditional' attitudes 78% (n=53) reported the woman as the main carer compared to 58% (n=119) of those with 'modern' attitudes. In addition those with more traditional attitudes were half as likely as those with more modern attitudes to report the man as the main carer. However even though those with more modern attitudes were less likely to report the

Table 9.11 BHPS 1991: Type of care used and who cares for children when ill by attitudes to women's role

	Attitudes held								Row	
	Traditional[a]	Mixed[b] traditional	Mixed[c] modern	Modern[d]	Traditional[a]	Mixed[b] traditional	Mixed[c] modern	Modern[d]	Freq	Total
	row %				col %	col %	col%	col%		
Type of care used*										
Home-based	(.2)	12	68	20	100	86	67	46	465	100
External/formal	—	(1)	45	54	—	(1)	9	26	97	13
External/informal	(.2)	(4)	64	32	—	(12)	23	28	174	24
Total									7 36	100
Who cares for ill children*										
Wife cares	(.2)	10	66	24	(100)	78	67	58	504	66
Husband cares	—	(5)	65	30	—	(6)	11	12	83	11
Other cares	—	(4)	59	37	—	(8)	17	26	143	18
Missing	—	—	—	—	—	(9)	5	(3)	36	5
Total									7 66	100

*   sig < .05

** sig < .001

Brackets denote cell sizes of fewer than 10 cases

'Other' carers include mothers help/nanny, relative, friend, neighbour or other person.

Base 100% = sample

a	Traditional	: type of care =	1	a who cares =	1
b	Mixed traditional	: type of care =	64	b who cares =	68
c	Mixed modern	: type of care =	471	c who cares =	492
d	Modern	: type of care =	200	d who cares =	205
			736		766

Table 9.12   BHPS 1991: Occupation, monthly gross pay and usual hours worked by attitudes held

	Traditional	Mixed traditional	Mixed modern	Modern	Freq	Total
				Attitudes held		
		row %				col %
Occupation*						
Professional/administrative	—	8	57	35	204	27
Clerical/craft	(.4)	11	60	28	211	28
Service/sales	(.1)	10	72	18	203	26
Plant op/other	—	5	70	25	145	19
Missing	—	—	—	—		3
—						
Total					766	100
Monthly gross pay**						
Up to £200	(.5)	12	73	14	151	24
£201 - £700	(.1)	8	67	25	331	52
£701 - £1000	—	(1)	66	33	68	11
£1001 - £1500	—	(5)	40	56	55	8
Over £1500	—	(6)	38	56	34	5
Total					638	100
Usual weekly hours**						
Under 16	(.4)	17	71	12	226	30
16 - 29	—	6	70	24	247	32
30 or more	(.1)	(5)	53	42	275	36
DK/missing	—	—	—	—	18	2
Total					766	100

*   *sig < .05*

**   *sig < .001*

Brackets denote cell sizes under ten cases

Monthly gross pay missing in 128 cases

6 cases with missing attitudinal items excluded

woman as the main carer, this responsibility did not necessarily pass to their male partner. Of those holding 'mixed modern' attitudes, 17% (n=84) said ill children were cared for by someone else such as a relative or childminder while 26% (n=54) of those with 'modern' attitudes said the same.

Table 9.12 gives the employment characteristics of respondents responsible for the care of children 12 and under by attitudes to women's employment and the home. Those in professional occupations were more likely to hold 'modern' attitudes. However the most significant relationships were with the level of earnings and number of hours worked. As the level of monthly gross pay rises so does the percentage of those holding 'modern' attitudes. Of respondents earning between £201 and £700 per month, 25% (n=82) held 'modern' attitudes compared with 56% (n=30) of those earning between £1001 and £1500 per month. A similar pattern can be seen with the number of hours worked, particularly at the divide between part-time and full-time employment. As the number of hours worked rises so does the percentage of those with 'modern' attitudes. Of respondents working fewer than sixteen hours per week 12%, (n=28) held 'modern' attitudes compared to 42% (n=115) of those working 30 hours or more per week. Occupation, level of earnings, hours of employment and attitudes to women's employment clearly influence the type of childcare used. In order to disentangle which factors are most significant a multi-variate analysis would be needed. The cost of childcare is a further element to be considered. For those with lower earnings in part-time employment the cost of childcare may act as a disincentive to greater participation in the labour market. These issues are considered in the following section.

Footnotes to Chapter 9

1. Note that 'mother' includes natural, step or adoptive mothers and mother figures such as a cohabiting   partner of a man with children from a previous relationship.

2. In 30 cases information on types of childcare used was not available.

3. As the numbers using a third type of childcare are relatively small these have not been reported.

4. Respondents with missing values were not included.

   Items were recoded so that the scale ran in the same direction for each statement, i.e. 1 = strongly disagree to 5 = strongly agree.

10. Cost of childcare

In 79% (n=611) of cases nothing was paid for childcare while 21% (n=161) did pay for some or all of their childcare[1]. Table 10.1 gives the household characteristics of those paying for some or all of their childcare and those not paying for childcare. Lone parents with children under five were most likely to pay for some or all of their childcare. Respondents who were members of dual-earner couples were also more likely to pay for some or all of their childcare. The age of the youngest child is also significantly related to whether care is paid or unpaid. Those with a youngest child of two or under were more likely to pay for their childcare than those with children of school age. Of those with children aged two or under 35% (n=75) used paid care compared to 12% (n=54) of those with a youngest child of between 5 and 15 years. The number of children present also influences whether care is paid or unpaid with those with one child being most likely to pay for some or all of their care.

Table 10.2 gives the employment characteristics of those paying or not paying for childcare. Occupation, monthly gross pay and usual hours worked are all significantly related to whether childcare is paid or unpaid. Those in professional occupations are most likely to pay for some or all of their childcare. Of those in professional occupations 35% (n=72) paid for some or all of their childcare compared with 10% (n=21) of those in personal service or sales occupations. As monthly gross pay rises so does the percentage of respondents paying for some or all of their childcare. The most striking difference is between those earning less than £700 per month and those earning more than £700 per month. Only 17% (n=55) of those earning between £201 and £700 per month paid for some or all of their childcare while 47% (n=33) of those earning between £701 and £1000 per month paid for some or all of their childcare. As the majority of respondents with dependent children aged twelve or under were earning less than £700 per month this suggests that for most people the cost of childcare may be considered to be prohibitive relative to their earnings. Interestingly, the level of household income did not have a marked effect on whether childcare was paid or unpaid which suggests that it is the earnings of the 'responsible adult' which are of greatest importance. When we consider the hours worked by whether childcare is paid or unpaid a similar pattern is clear. As the hours of work increase so does the percentage of those paying for some or all of their childcare with the most marked change being at the divide between part-time and full-time employment. Of those working between 16 and 29 hours per week 14% (n=35) paid for some or all of their care while 35% (n=97) of those working 30 hours or more paid for some or all of their childcare. However, what is striking throughout Tables 10.1 and 10.2 are the relatively high percentages of respondents not paying for any of their childcare, something which is apparent across household types and differing employment situations.

When we cross-tabulate whether care is paid or unpaid by the type of childcare used 22% (n=134) of those not paying for the first type of childcare mentioned gave an external/informal type of care while 77% (n=470) used a home-based type of unpaid care (see Table 10.3). Of the 126 respondents who reported an amount paid for the first mentioned type of care, 71% (n=89) gave an external/formal type and 29% (n=37) an external/informal type of care. On the type of care mentioned second, 56% (n=108) of those who did not pay for care said they used an external/informal type. However 55% (n=36) of those paying for the second mentioned type of care also used an external/informal type of care. The use of relatives or friends for childcare cannot therefore be assumed to be unpaid care in all cases.

Of those who paid for some or all of their childcare 47% (n=71) paid under £20 per week in total, 27% (n=31) paid a total of between £21 and £40 per week while 26% (n=40) paid over £40 per week in total. The mean weekly cost of childcare was £31, but the cost of external/informal types of care was significantly cheaper than external/formal types of care. Table 10.4 gives the weekly cost of childcare by the type of care used. As we can see 58% (n=28) of those paying under £20 per week used an external/informal type of care as their first mentioned type compared with 92% (n=36) of those paying over £40 per week for external/formal types of care. The number of dependent children did not have any significant effect on the amount paid for childcare, possibly because paid care was most common where there was one child only. The cost of childcare was significantly related to the age of the youngest child with 78% (n=30) of those paying over £40 per week having a child aged two or under (see Table 10.5).

Respondents paying for all or some of their childcare were asked who paid for this care. In 92% (n=100) of cases the 'responsible adult' paid for all or most of the care out of her/his wages, in 6% (n=48) the cost was shared with the spouse or partner and in 2% (n=12) of cases the spouse or partner paid for all or most of the care. We should remember that 98% of

Table 10.1   BHPS 1991: Household characteristics of those paying/not paying for childcare

	Some/all paid row %	None paid row %	Total Freq	Total col %
Household type**				
Dual-earner/child <5	33	67	244	32
Dual-earner/child 5-12	11	89	347	45
Sole-earner/child <5	30	70	39	5
Sole-earner/child 5-12	—	100	46	6
Lone parent/child <5	44	56	28	4
Lone parent/child 5-12	26	74	63	8
Missing	—	—	10	—
Total			772	100
Age of youngest child**				
0 - 2	35	65	214	28
3 - 4	29	71	96	12
5 - 12	12	88	455	60
Missing	—	—	7	—
Total			772	100
Number of children*				
One	28	72	283	37
Two	17	83	359	46
Three	16	84	110	14
Four or more	(11)	89	20	3
Total			772	100

*   sig < .01

**   sig < .001

Brackets denote cell size under ten cases

'responsible adults' were women, with the implication being that women who take on paid employment also bear the responsibility for paying for any childcare required. There were no significant relationships between who paid for care and employment characteristics or attitudes to women's employment. The only significant relationship was with the level of household income. As household income rose there was a greater tendency for respondents to say they shared the cost of childcare with their partner (see Table 10.6). This suggests that it is women in low income households who are least able to pay for their childcare who find themselves in the position of doing so if other forms of unpaid care are not available.

Table 10.2   BHPS 1991: Employment characteristics of those paying/not paying for childcare

	Some/all paid row %	None paid row %	Total Freq	col %
Occupation**				
Professional/administative	35	65	205	27
Clerical/craft	28	72	212	28
Service/sales	10	90	207	27
Other	(6)	94	145	18
Missing	—	—	3	—
Total			772	100
Monthly gross pay**				
Up to £200	7	93	151	24
£201 - £700	17	83	332	52
£701 - £1000	47	53	70	11
£1001 - £1500	46	54	55	8
Over £1500	49	51	34	5
Total			642	100
Usual weekly hours**				
Under 16	11	89	226	29
16 - 29	14	86	250	33
30 or more	35	65	277	36
DK/missing/NA	16	84	19	2
Total			772	100

** sig < .001

Information on monthly gross pay missing in 130 cases

Table 10.3   BHPS 1991: Whether childcare unpaid or paid by types of care used

	Types of care used			Total	
	Home-based	Formal row %	Informal	Freq	col %
1st type mentioned					
Unpaid	77	(1)	22	611	83
Paid	—	71	29	126	17
Total				737	100
2nd type mentioned					
Unpaid	43	(.4)	56	192	75
Paid	—	45	55	65	25
Total				257	100

Base n=737

35 cases with missing information excluded

Brackets denote cell sizes under ten cases

Table 10.4   BHPS 1991: Total weekly cost of childcare by type of paid childcare used

| | Types of paid care | | Total | |
| | Formal | Informal | | |
	row %	row %	Freq	col %
Weekly cost				
1st type mentioned**				
Under £20	42	58	48	38
£21 - £40	85	(15)	36	28
Over £40	92	(8)	38	31
DK\missing	—	—	4	3
Total			126	100
2nd type mentioned				
Under £20	47	53	34	53
£21 - £40	(42)	(58)	14	21
Over £40	(50)	(50)	12	18
DK\missing	—	—	5	8
Total			65	100

**   *sig < .001*

Brackets denote cell sizes under ten cases

Table 10.5   BHPS 1991: Age of youngest child

| | 0-2 | 3-4 | 5-12 | Total | |
		row %		Freq	col %
Weekly cost					
1st type mentioned**					
Under £20	29	(15)	54	48	38
£21 - £40	61	15	(23)	36	28
Over £40 missing	78	(14)	(8)	38	31
DK/missing	—	—	—	4	3
Total				126	100

**   *sig < .001*

Brackets denote cell sizes under ten cases

Table 10.6   HPS 1991: Monthly household income by who pays for childcare

Monthly household income	Who pays for care		
	All/most from own wages	Shared with partner	Partner pays all/most
	%	%	%
Up to £500	(3)	—	—
£501 - £1000	15	—	(8)
£1001 - £150	17	(10)	—
£1501 - £2000	24	28	(25)
£2001 - £3000	24	46	(17)
Over £3000	17	(16)	(50)
Base = 100%	76	39	11

**   sig < .05

Base n=149

Brackets denote cell sizes under ten cases

Footnotes to Chapter 10

1. Note that of the 161 respondents who said they paid for some or all of their childcare information on the amount paid was reported in 126 cases only.

11 Child carers - conclusion

In conclusion the data suggest that women continue to bear the main responsibility for the care of dependent children with consequent effects upon their labour market behaviour. Although some respondents are adopting strategies to fit in with their spouse's working hours or with children's school hours, these enable mainly part-time rather than full-time employment to be undertaken. When we look at the use of childcare it is striking how many working women rely on home-based types of care and the relatively small numbers using external/formal types of care which must be paid for. As the Women and Employment Survey (WES) of 1980 found, the arrangements women make for childcare vary with the number of hours worked. Although those in full-time employment were more likely to use external/formal types of care than those in part-time employment, home-based and external/ informal types of care were more commonly used by all women, a pattern which is confirmed by the BHPS data. There is therefore little indication of change in the types of childcare used by employed women in the intervening decade between the two surveys. The numbers relying on either free or relatively cheap care provided by a relative or friend is also marked suggesting that for many women it is access to this type of external/informal care which makes taking on paid employment financially viable. In the WES only 16% of women paid anything for their childcare compared to 21% of respondents in the BHPS data. As WES found the age of children and the number of hours being worked also influenced whether care was paid or unpaid. The BHPS data confirm this pattern but also suggest that the percentage of women paying for childcare has increased. In the WES 48% of those working full-time with pre-school age children paid for care while only 7% of those working part-time with school-age children paid for care. In the BHPS 56% of those working full-time with pre-school age children paid for care while 9% of those working part-time with school age children aged 12 or under paid for care. In addition 35% of those with children aged two or under paid for childcare and 29% of those with children aged three or four paid for care. While those working full-time were more likely to to pay for childcare the majority, 65%, relied on unpaid types of care while they were working. Despite the growth in recent years of women with children re-entering paid employment or maintaining a continuous presence within the labour market throughout their childrearing years, the data suggest that childcare responsibilities continue to affect women's employment experience.

References

Brannen, J. and Moss, P. (1987) 'Dual Earner Households: Women's Financial Contributions After the Birth of the First Child' in Brannen, J and Wilson, G (eds) *Give and Take in Families* London, Allen and Unwin.

Bone, M. (1977) 'Pre-school Children and the Need for Daycare' *OPCS Report*, HMSO, London.

Bridgwood, A and Savage, D (1993) *General Household Survey*, Series GHS No 22, HMSO London

Cohen, B. (1988) 'Caring For Children: services and policies for childcare and equal opportunities in the United Kingdom'. *Report for the European Commission's Childcare Network*, Family Policy Studies Centre, London.

Cohen, B. (1990) 'Caring for Children. The 1990 Report'. *Report for the European Commission's Childcare Network, on Childcare Services and Policy in the UK*. Family Policy Studies Centre, Occasional Paper series, London.

Dex, S. (1986) 'Women's Labour Supply and the Demand for Child Care Provision in The Women and Employment Survey', *Report to the Equal Opportunities Commission*, London (unpublished).

Dex, S. (1987) *Women's Occupational Mobility: a lifetime perspective.* London, Macmillan.

Joshi, H. (ed) (1989) *The Changing Population of Britain*, Oxford, Basil Blackwell.

Martin, J. and Roberts, C. (1984) *Women and Employment. A lifetime perspective.* DE/OPCS, HMSO.

Moss, P. (1990) 'Childcare in the European Community, 1985-1990', *Women of Europe*, supplements No 31, (August), European Commission Childcare Network, Brussels.

Appendix A

SOC divisions used in BHPS analysis

Because the BHPS 1991 sample contain a small number of carers in employment, the SOC major groups have been aggregated as follows:

1. Managers and administrators; Professional occupations; Associate professional and technical occupations.
2. Clerical and secretarial occupations; Craft and related occupations.
3. Personal and protective service occupations; Sales occupations; Plant and machine operatives; Other occupations.

Appendix B

Major SIC Divisions (revised 1980)

0   Agriculture, forestry and fishing.
1   Energy and water supply industries.
2   Extraction of minerals and ores other than fuels; manufacture of metals, mineral products and chemicals.
3   Metal goods, engineering and vehicle industries.
4   Other manufacturing industries.
5   Construction.
6   Distribution, hotels and catering; repairs.
7   Transport and communication.
8   Banking, finance, insurance.
9   Other services.

Because BHPS 1991 sample contains a small number of carers in employment, the ten major SIC divisions have been aggregated as follows:

1. Energy - includes divisions 0 and 1.
2. Manufacturing - includes divisions 2, 3 and 4.
3. Construction - division 5.
4. Services - includes divisions 6, 7, 8 and 9.

Appendix C

Attitudes to women and employment

Respondents in the BHPS answered a short self-completion questionnaire which included a series of attitudinal questions about family, work and women's employment. Respondents were asked whether they agreed or disagreed with a series of statements on a five-point scale from 'strongly agree' to 'strongly disagree'. The statements used in this analysis were as follows:

A pre-school child is likely to suffer if his or her mother works.

All in all, family life suffers when the women has a full-time job.

A woman and her family would all be happier is she goes out to work.

Both the husband and wife should contribute to the household income.

Having a full-time job is the best way for a woman to be an independent person.

A husband's job is to earn money; a wife's job is to look after the home and family.

Employers should make special arrangements to help mothers combine jobs and childcare.

A single parent can bring up children as well as a couple.

EMPLOYMENT DEPARTMENT
RESEARCH SERIES

The Research Series of reports was introduced in March 1992 and supersedes the Department's Research Papers (covering employment and industrial relations issues) and the Training Research and Development series.

Listed below are the current reports in the new series. Copies can be obtained free of charge from Research Management Branch, Employment Department, Room W441, Moorfoot, Sheffield S1 4PQ or by contacting our Orderline telephone number 0742 593932.

Listings of Research Papers and Training Research and Development reports can be obtained by contacting the above address or telephone number.

RES

No.   Title and author(s)

1. **Measure for Measure**

   A comparative analysis of measures to combat racial discrimination in the member states of the European Community. I Forbes and G Mead, Equal Opportunities Study Group, University of Southampton. 1992.

2. **New Developments in Employee Involvement**

   M Marchington, J Goodman, A Wilkinson and P Ackers, Manchester School of Management, UMIST. 1992.

3. **Entrepreneurship in Cleveland 1979-1989: A Study of the Effects of the Enterprise Culture**

   D J Storey and A Strange, Centre for Small and Medium Sized Enterprises, Warwick Business School, University of Warwick. 1992.

4. **Alcohol Consumption and Sickness Absence: An Analysis of 1984 General Household Survey Data.**

   L M Joeman, Employment Department. 1992.

5. **Payment Systems: A Look at Current Practices.**

   B Casey, J Lakey and M White, Policy Studies Institute. September 1992.

6. **New Inward Investment and the Northern Region Labour Market.**

   F Peck and I Stone, Newcastle Economic Research Unit, University of Northumbria at Newcastle. October 1992.

7. **Final-Offer Arbitration in the UK: Incidence, processes and outcomes.**

   S Milner, Centre for Economic Performance, London School of Economics. January 1993.

8. **Information Requirements in Occupational Decision Making**

   Dr N C Boreham and Dr T A A Arthur, University of Manchester. March 1993.

9. **The Motivation to Train**

   M Crowder and K Pupynin, Minds at Work. April 1993.

10. **TEC Participation in National Development Activity**

    Ernst & Young. May 1993.

11. **Business Growth Training Option 3 Evaluation Project**

   J. Neill Marshall, Neil Alderman, Cecilia Wong and Alfred Thwaites, Centre for Urban and Regional Development Studies, University of Newcastle.   May 1993.

12. **TECs & employers: Developing effective links. Part 1: a survey.**

   Patrick Vaughan, Employment Department. July 1993.

13. **TECs & employers: Developing effective links. Part 2: TEC-employer links in six TEC areas.**

   Theresa Crowley-Bainton, Policy Studies Institute. August 1993.

14. **The Abolition of the Dock Labour Scheme.**

   N Evans and D MacKay, Pieda plc and M Garratt and P Sutcliffe, MDS Transmodal. September 1993.

15. **New firm formation and small business growth in the United Kingdom: Spatial and temporal variations and determinants**

   D Keeble and S Walker, Department of Geography and Small Business Research Centre, University of Cambridge, and M Robson, Department of Economics, University of Newcastle-upon-Tyne. September 1993.

16. **Employment Policies for Disabled People: A review of legislation and services in fifteen countries**

   N Lunt and P Thornton, Social Policy Research Unit, University of York. October 1993.

17. **An Evaluation of Supported Employment Initiatives for Disabled People**

   A Pozner and J Hammond, OUTSET Consultancy Services (with a contribution by V Tannam, Employment Service). October 1993.

18. **Teleworking in Britain**

   Ursula Huws, Analytica. October 1993.

19. **Partnerships for Equality: A review of Employers' Equal Opportunities Groups**

   G Whitting, J Moore and P Warren, ECOTEC Research and Consulting Ltd. October 1993.

20. **Factors Influencing Individual Committment to Lifetime Learning**

   Malcolm Maguire, Susan Maguire and Alan Felstead, Centre for Labour Market Studies, University of Leicester. December 1993.

21. **Investors in People. A qualitative study of employers.**

   A Rix, R Parkinson and R Gaunt, CRG People at Work. January 1994.

22. **The 1992 Survey of Industrial Tribunal Applications**

   Nigel Tremlett, Social and Community Planning Research (SCPR) and Nitya Banerji, Employment Department. February 1994.

23. **Thinking and Learning at Work: A report on the development and evaluation of the Thinking Skills At Work modules**

   Nigel Blagg, Rachel Lewis and Marj Ballinger, Nigel Blagg Associates. March 1994.

24. **The Early Use of Local Initiative Funds by TECs: Evoking local prosperity**

   John Bazalgette, David Armstrong, Jean Hutton and Colin Quine, The Grubb Institute. March 1994.

25. **Regional Advice Units: An examination of models for delivering advice and guidance to TECs and Department of Employment Regional Offices**

   Kate Pupynin and Mary Crowder, Minds at Work. April 1994.

26. **The Role of Evaluation in TEC Planning: Final report**

   Ian Pearson, WMEB Consultants. April 1994.

27. **The Changing Structure of Occupations and Earnings in Great Britain, 1975-1990. An analysis based on the New Earnings Survey Panel Dataset.**

   P Elias and M Gregory, Institute for Employment Research, University of Warwick. May 1994.

28. **Middle Managers: Their Contribution to Employee Involvement**

   M Fenton O'Creevy and N Nicholson, Centre for Organisational Research, London Business School. June 1994.

29. **An International Overview of Employment Policies and Practices Towards Older Workers**

J Moore, B Tilson and G Whitting, ECOTEC Research and Consulting Ltd. June 1994.

30. **Training: An exploration of the word and the concept with an analysis of the implications for survey design**

P Campanelli with Roger Thomas, Survey Methods Centre, SCPR, and J Channell with L McAulay and A Renouf, Research & Development Unit for English Studies, University of Birmingham. July 1994.

31. **Individual Commitment to Lifetime Learning: Individuals' Attitudes. Report on the qualitative phase.**

S Taylor and L Spencer, Social and Community Planning Research (SCPR). July 1994.

32. **Individual Commitment to Lifetime Learning: Individuals' Attitudes. Report on the quantitative survey.**

A Park, Social and Community Planning Research (SCPR). July 1994.

33. **Sunday Working. Analysis of an Employer Survey.**

Prof. D Bosworth, Manchester School of Management, UMIST. August 1994.

34. **The Economic Effects of Reductions in Working Hours: the UK Engineering Industry.**

R Richardson and M Rubin, Department of Industrial Relations and Centre for Economic Performance, London School of Economics. September 1994.

35. **Participation and Progress in the Labour Market: Key issues for women.**

L Spencer and S Taylor, Social and Community Planning Research (SCPR). September 1994.

36. **Acting Positively: Positive action under the Race Relations Act 1976.**

C Welsh, J Knox and M Brett, Capita Management Consultancy. October 1994.

37. **The Impact of the Posted Workers' Directive on Company Practice in the United Kingdom.**

M Gold, National Institute of Economic and Social Research. October 1994.

38. **Thematic Evaluation of EHEI.**

C Biggs, R Brighton, P Minnitt, R Pow and W Wicksteed, Segal Quince Wicksteed Ltd. October 1994.

39. **Caring and Employment**

L Corti, H Laurie and S Dex, ESRC Research Centre on Micro-social Change, University of Essex. November 1994.